TEVYA
AND HIS
DAUGHTERS

BY ARNOLD PERL

Based on the Tevya stories of Sholom Aleichem

★

★

DRAMATISTS
PLAY SERVICE
INC.

TEVYA AND HIS DAUGHTERS was first presented by Banner Productions (Howard Da Silva—Sanford Friedman—Arnold Perl—Myron Weinberg) at the Carnegie Hall Playhouse, New York City, on September 16, 1957. The play was directed by Howard Da Silva, music composed by Serge Hovey, setting by Howard Bay. The original cast, in order of appearance, was:

TEVYA	Mike Kellin
GOLDE, *his wife*	Anna Vita Berger
TZEITL, *his oldest daughter*	Joan Harvey
HODEL, *his second daughter*	Carroll Conroy
CHAVA, *his third daughter*	Anne Fielding
RICH WOMAN	Ruth Kaner
RICH WOMAN'S DAUGHTER	Ellen Holly
RICH MERCHANT	William Myers
LAZAR WOLF	Gilbert Green
MOTTEL KAMZOIL	Conrad Bromberg
FEFERAL PERCHIK	Paul E. Richards
RABBI	William Myers

ACT I

PART 1: How Tevya Became a Dairyman.
PART 2: Tzeitl.

ACT II

Hodel.

The action takes place in and around Tevya's house, a poor hut in Czarist Russia at the turn of the century.

NOTES ON THE SET

No set, as such, is needed. The action can be played against a neutral background, or drapes.

The set pieces are simple. Tevya's house at L. boasts a rickety, well-worn table D. S., three or four stools, a small shelf for plates, knives and forks and a modest samovar. Upstage of these elements is the bed-on-top-of-oven, on which Golde and Tevya sleep. The daughters' beds are offstage.

Tevya's wagon at C. can be made of anything convenient. A bench can be used. Two stools will serve—for himself and his passengers. A platform (4 x 4) having two steps front and back will serve as Tevya's wagon and as a set piece (over which Tevya dances when drunk; over which Feferal exits; which is used for the wedding ceremony and later as part of the succah Tevya builds).

Lazar Wolf's, at R., shows a well-made heavy (small) table, two well-built chairs, a brass samovar, a suggestion of hanging copperware, a small sideboard on which the samovar and the bottle of schnapps rest.

The Rich Merchant's area, at R., can use the sideboard from Lazar Wolf's (without its being moved). The suggestion of a festive table comes from a lit candle, a few plates. It may be helpful to play the Merchant scene on a platform (6" to 8" high) behind the Lazar Wolf area.

Tevya's barn needs no dressing. It can be the area downstage R. of Tevya's wagon.

For Act II, strike the Lazar Wolf table, chairs and sideboard.

Tevya and His Daughters

ACT I

PART 1

HOW TEVYA BECAME A DAIRYMAN

Tevya crosses the darkened stage, from R. to L., carrying an armful of food in packages. He is 50, a drayman, and wearing his Sabbath "best," which is to say his week-day best, that is his work clothes. Now he stands, at midnight, just outside his house, L., arms laden, in a state of exultation. A miracle has happened.

TEVYA. O, Lord, with all the troubles of the Universe on your back, accept thanks for the blessings of this night. It's me, Tevya the Drayman, with the mud on his wagon, his horse and himself. A man. But as is written a man may be in the mud, but he's never of the mud; he may be down but he's never extinguished; as long as your teeth are chattering, dear Lord, you're alive. And this night Thou hast performed a miracle, and as the Bible tells us, Let there be light. *(Lights slowly come on.)* Let there also be celebration. Golde, children, everyone! Arise, awake, a mazeltov and a holiday! Everybody come. *(Lights reveal the interior of Tevya's mansion at L.: a poor Jewish hut in Russia, in the latter part of the 19th century. The furniture is rough, bare and well-used. Golde, his wife, and his three eldest daughters, Tzeitl, Hodel and Chava, enter sleepily L.)* As King David said, Prepare for there came a day: That day has come. *(The girls rush into his arms in happy anticipation.)*
GOLDE. Do you know what time it is?
TEVYA. Get the white tablecloth, set the table.
GOLDE. Have you gone out of your mind?

5

TEVYA. Mazeltov, my darlings; mazeltov, Golde. (*He kisses all the girls and tries to kiss Golde.*)

GOLDE. An endless mazeltov to you.

TEVYA. Get the dishes; more candles!

GOLDE. What are we celebrating, my beloved breadwinner in rags? (*Tevya reveals the food he has been carrying.*)

TEVYA. Behold soup with noodles, behold roast beef, stuffed goose's neck, kishka, herring, sturgeon! Why are you standing around? Get the platters and the forks. My jaws have been aching for an hour to get at it. (*He draws a bottle from inside his shirt.*) Plus wine, fit for King Solomon himself.

GOLDE. (*Looking and smelling, but not believing her eyes.*) Tell me, my helpmate, what insane benefactor has decided to feed the countryside including Tevya and his seven daughters?

TEVYA. I'll tell everything. Only, first, Hodel, heat up the samovar. Get the glasses for tea. And we will celebrate our Independence; because, Golde, hold out your nightgown. (*Golde has grown silent. Scattering a pile of bills into her apron.*) Look. One's, two's, even three-ruble notes! Count —— (*Golde cries and counts to herself.*)

HODEL. Mother, why are you crying? Mama.

TEVYA. I'll explain. When your heart is full, your eyes run over. It relieves the pressure. Your mother is thinking as follows. Tevya is a drayman, she is thinking, with a wagon and half a horse. What does he do all day? Hauls wood from the forest to the railroad station for, I'm ashamed to admit it, half a ruble a day. And not every day; right, Golde? (*Golde cries louder.*) I'm on the right track. So, asks your mother, my Golde, where would Tevya get such a fortune? (A little glass, please, Tzeitl.) Where? He sold his soul to the devil? I didn't. He turned into a highway robber and held up one of the rich merchants who is in our neck of the woods? Wrong twice. No, Golde, listen. Dry your eyes and listen to your schlimazl of a husband. This is food and drink and money that has come to Tevya honestly because of his labor and on account of his wits.

GOLDE. Thirty-seven rubles! (*She wails.*)

HODEL. Oh, mama, that's no reason to carry on.

TEVYA. Let her cry. She has, your blessed mother, something to worry about. A house that leaks, a kitchen forever empty, a husband that is not the First Provider on earth, and seven —— (*He

6

counts them off.) One, two, three—where are the little ones? Ah, don't wake them; we'll save theirs for the morning. So with seven daughters, seven to marry off, she is entitled to her tears. As King Solomon tells us in the Prophets ——

GOLDE. Never mind the quotation, what happened?

TEVYA. Sit down, eat, satisfy your hunger, wash it down with a little tea, and I will tell you how Tevya made his fortune. Oh, I forgot —— (*He leaps up.*) We have a cow. And better than a cow, a cow that, perhaps, gives milk.

GOLDE. Begin at the beginning. (*During the following reenactment. Tevya moves stage R. Golde and the girls are all stage L. and remain there throughout the following "story." Tevya is in the room with them, telling the story as it happened. As other people enter the story, they relate to Tevya stage R. But Tevya can, and does, turn from the people of the story and speak to his wife and children. Light on Golde and the children diminishes.*)

TEVYA. This afternoon, there is, as usual, no work. The horse and I are walking, both in the dust, for why should I tax the poor animal and make him carry me ——?

GOLDE. Tevya!

TEVYA. As I said, we're walking and thinking. That is, I'm thinking, the horse is only walking. I'm thinking, eight months, eight, that is, not including the horse, who, after all, can't be satisfied with a quotation from the Talmud.

GOLDE. Tevya!!

TEVYA. So it's time for the Afternoon Prayer and I begin to recite. "Blessed are they who dwell in Thy House, O Lord. (Thy House, I take it, is somewhat more spacious than mine.) Thou raiseth up them that are bowed down. (Surely, by now it's getting close to my turn.)" (*To Golde.*) And just as I'm finishing the last blessing I see them.

GOLDE. Who?

TEVYA. Two mysterious creatures are approaching stealthily and I remember the thieves that are all over the forest. I think I'll say a prayer. What's the good, I answer, I just finished a prayer and here they are. So I jump in the wagon. I crack the whip. I holler giddyap ——

GOLDE. And?

TEVYA. The horse is nibbling. He doesn't notice me. And the two terrors are upon me. (*Tevya covers his head as Two Women ap-*

proach him from ·R., an elderly woman and her young daughter. His eyes tight closed.) If it's gold you're after, you've got the wrong man.

OLDER WOMAN. Calm yourself, my good man, and open your eyes. We are two women, visitors from Kiev. We are staying in Boiberik. We went for a walk and got lost.

YOUNG WOMAN. Can you tell us the way to Boiberik?

TEVYA. Of course I can tell you the way to Boiberik. I am Tevya, the Drayman, and the way to Boiberik is the road I travel every day.

YOUNG WOMAN. Is it far?

TEVYA. Far to some is near. If, to give an instance, it is a load of wood to haul from here to Boiberik, for me it's far. If you're paying for the load, for you it's near.

OLDER WOMAN. How far, my good man?

TEVYA. Now there's a fair question. A few miles, maybe eight. *(The women are alarmed at the distance.)*

YOUNG WOMAN. That's terrible.

TEVYA. I'm sorry it's so far. If it was up to me, I'd bring it closer. But the Lord in Heaven who planted Boiberik didn't consult Tevya.

OLDER WOMAN. Now listen, my good man, we are tired and cannot take another step. All day long we have had only a glass of coffee, a little fish, some rolls and butter ——

TEVYA. On such a diet, you cannot expect a person to dance.

YOUNG WOMAN. *(Winningly.)* Couldn't you take us to Boiberik?

OLDER WOMAN. That's exactly the idea.

TEVYA. It is a fine idea, with this exception. I am coming from Boiberik, and you are going to Boiberik. As the Talmud states you can't go in two directions at the same time.

YOUNG WOMAN. A wise and learned man like yourself, who can quote Scripture, can surely figure that out. Turn your wagon around, move over so we can get in and there's your answer.

TEVYA. That's one answer. Another is Giddyap and I'm gone.

OLDER WOMAN. My good man, we shall see to it that your kindness is rewarded.

TEVYA. "Rewarded" is an excellent word. Perhaps it means thank you, very much? *(Turns toward Golde and the girls.)* And before I know it, they interpret that question as an invitation and they

8

are crowding in the wagon with me. (*The two women have come around until they are sitting on either side of Tevya. He turns back to them.*)

OLDER WOMAN. Let us not dally here all day, Reb Tevya.

TEVYA. I'm sorry but the horse doesn't want to play.

YOUNG WOMAN. The whip, Tevya; use the whip.

TEVYA. Thanks for the suggestion, but my friend, the horse, is as used to the whip as I am to poverty. Whup—there he goes. (*They jog along with the horse.*)

OLDER WOMAN. Is this as fast as he goes?

TEVYA. To answer you directly, you're lucky he started. This is Tevya's horse and he knows this is not the way home. For him this is the way to work. So be content he's moving. (*To Golde.*) We jog along—up, down, around, finally I ask. (*Turns back to the women.*) Tell me, since we're nearby, where do you wish to be dropped off?

OLDER WOMAN. My dear man, what kind of language is that? We don't wish to be dropped off anywhere.

TEVYA. I beg your pardon. "Dropped off" is an expression among logs. Among genteel folks we say where do you wish to be transported, dear ladies, when, with God's help and the Blessings of Providence, we finally arrive at our destination? Where in Boiberik?

OLDER WOMAN. Why didn't you say so in the first place?

TEVYA. As the saying goes—It is better to ask twice than to go wrong.

YOUNG WOMAN. Are you familiar with the Green Datcha with the black trim?

TEVYA. Oh, the millionaire's! Do me a favor, please. If you are connected with anyone living there, tell the master of the house that Tevya with the wagon is something of a pauper.

YOUNG WOMAN. Mother, we're here —— (*A babble of offstage voices is heard R. as the two women rush into the arms of their family.*)

VOICES. Grandma! Mother! Auntie! We thought wolves! We were so worried! What happened? Mazeltov! (*And Tevya is left alone. From his position "in the wagon" he turns and addresses Golde.*)

TEVYA. They rush onto the porch. Hugging and kissing and blessing God and there I see such a spread—everything in the

9

world there is to eat. And I am standing at a distance, listening to all the mazeltovs and smelling all the smells and saying Tevya, you are forgotten. Tevya, you're a fool, a schlimazl —— (*A Merchant, the head of the house, comes out* R. *as Tevya is saying this to Golde.*)

THE MERCHANT. Where's the schlimazl? Where is he? Oh, there you are.

TEVYA. Yes, sir; it's me. Here, in the dark.

MERCHANT. Let's have a look at you. Come on in. Maybe you'd like a little whiskey, a drop of schnappes?

TEVYA. A little whiskey? What does the Talmud say? God is good, but schnappes is something you can drink. (*Tevya and the Merchant are joined by the two women and others at the datcha. A festive table is seen. Handed his drink.*) L'chaim.

MERCHANT. Long life. Tell us about yourself. Do you have children?

TEVYA. (*His drink finished.*) To answer you truthfully, sir, do I have children? If it is true that each child is worth a million, then I am richer by several millions than the richest in Boiberik. The only trouble is with all my wealth we still go to bed hungry. But as the saying goes, If you have enough girls, the whole world whirls. And I have enough. Seven. However, I am not complaining. For God is the Father; He has his way. He sits on high; I struggle below. My grandmother, may she rest in peace, used to say—If we didn't have to eat, we'd all be rich. I'll take another drop.

MERCHANT. (*Nodding and laughing.*) All right, give the man what he deserves. Help yourself, Reb Tevya. Take what you like —fowl, giblets, fish—take what you want.

TEVYA. You mean me?

MERCHANT. Of course, of course. Won't you take something?

TEVYA. A sick person you ask, a healthy one you give ——

MERCHANT. (*Expansively.*) Go ahead; why wait?

TEVYA. Excuse me, but don't expect me to sit down and start packing away such a spread when my wife and my seven are in bed without supper.

MERCHANT. You're a fine man, Reb Tevya. Mother, fix a bundle of food for Reb Tevya and his wife and his seven daughters. Enough for all of them. (*Turns to Tevya.*) Now tell me, what do you want for yourself?

10

TEVYA. What you're doing—that's fine.

MERCHANT. Now, now—don't be shy. What do you want for *yourself*? You know what I'm talking about.

TEVYA. Well, how do I know what what I did is worth?

MERCHANT. Whatever you think. You tell me how much. It's yours. (*Tevya turns from the Merchant in his dilemma and speaks to Golde.*)

TEVYA. Now this is the worst moment. If I said one ruble when he might have been ready to give me two, what will I do? I'll kill myself. On the other hand, suppose I said two rubles and he thinks I'm greedy and throws me out. I'll kill myself again. So, I take a deep breath and —— (*Tevya takes a deep breath and—in a small voice*) Three rubles, please. (*The Merchant and the others laugh.*) Too much? Too little? Excuse me if I said the wrong thing. After all a horse who has four legs stumbles once in a while. Why shouldn't a man who has only one tongue?

MERCHANT. (*Laughing.*) Put that food in his wagon. Here, Reb Tevya. Take this. Count it when you get home. It's more than three rubles, I can tell you.

OLDER WOMAN. (*Approaches.*) My good man, I want to give you something else. I have a cow. A milk cow. She used to be a wonderful milker —— 24 glasses a day—until someone cast an evil eye on her and you can't milk her any more.

TEVYA. That's all right.

OLDER WOMAN. You can milk her, but what I mean is, nothing comes.

TEVYA. Don't worry. We'll not only milk her, we'll get cream. My Golde knows how to make noodles out of nothing. To this she adds water and produces noodle soup. Every week she performs a miracle: we have food on the table for the Sabbath. So we'll take the cow. Thank you; bless you —— (*The Merchant and the others fade out R. and Tevya turns, finishing his story, toward Golde. By the end of his next speech, Golde and the girls are in the room with him, fully lit.*) I thanked them. I blessed them, I raced back and I can't eat another bite.

TZEITL. It's wonderful, Papa.

HODEL. Mama, you're still crying.

GOLDE. I had a dream about my Grandmother Tzeitl, for whom you, my oldest, are named. Just before your father came, I dreamed my grandmother, may she rest in peace, carried toward me a milkpail, filled to the brim.

TZEITL. You see, mama, it's a sign ——

GOLDE. Only she carried the pail *under* her apron to shield it from the evil eye.

HODEL. Oh, Mama, you don't believe that ——

TEVYA. Exactly. Superstition. Bubbemeise. An old woman's story. Not tonight. Let your Grandmother Tzeitl be happy in the true world, in Paradise. We all have this plus a cow.

GOLDE. I can't get the sight out of my eyes.

TEVYA. (*Who well knows how to distract her.*) Tell me, my darling, what shall we do with our fortune? First, what shall we do with the cow? What is your opinion?

GOLDE. The cow is simple. We'll drink the milk; we'll make the butter. What we don't eat, we'll sell.

TEVYA. And the money?

GOLDE. The money is something else. 37 rubles is a responsibility.

TEVYA. I've been thinking. Maybe if we bought a pair of horses ——

GOLDE. Horses get lame, my thinker.

TEVYA. How about a grocery store near Boiberik?

GOLDE. There are eleven groceries in Boiberik. Eight are starving and two just went bankrupt.

TEVYA. I'll go to the grain market in Odessa —— Do you know what's going on in Odessa these days?

GOLDE. In Odessa they have the Plague.

TEVYA. Your second-cousin-once-removed, Menachem Mendel, told me how in Kiev on mortgages alone ——

GOLDE. My second-cousin-once-removed is a luftmensch who lives on air and pipe dreams. Since he has been in business (forty-one years), he has amassed one thing: old age.

TEVYA. So what will we do with our wealth if you're so intelligent?

GOLDE. First, girls, to bed. Put away the celebration and to bed. (*The girls protest, then go.*) Take a look around you, Tevya. The mansion we live in. The chair. What we use for a table. And peek into the other room. For one night your seven daughters have been fed—congratulations! But you still have seven daughters. Seven arrangements to be arranged; seven dowries to be dowered; seven

12

still, in one word, to get married. So therefore we'll take the cow (if it is a cow) and buy us another cow. With the two, we will have milk and cream and butter and cheese. And with the girls and me to make it and you to sell it, we'll try to make a living from the rich who come to spend the summer in Boiberik ——

TEVYA. Such a head. (*He kisses her.*) You're right. As is written, Man is wise, but the ways of a woman —— So Tevya the Drayman is now Tevya the Dairyman. And he will work and work and, the Lord willing, take care of his girls and his wife and himself.

GOLDE. Already he's a Dairyman.

TEVYA. I mean it. For the first time in my life, I think, I'm beginning to see a little light.

GOLDE. Look yonder, you'll see light. Real light. It's dawn.

TEVYA. Already?

GOLDE. If I hadn't cut you off with the tracts and the citations, it would have been noon. All right, Dairyman, the day of labor has begun.

TEVYA. Such excitement, I'm dead on my feet. Let me lay down for an hour, and, God willing, get back some strength.

GOLDE. It'll be daylight in half an hour.

TEVYA. That's what I said. Half an hour. Then Tevya the Dairyman begins a new life. (*FADE OUT.*)

CURTAIN

ACT I

Part 2

TZEITL

Tevya is seen driving his horse along the road at c. The MUSIC is spirited.

TEVYA. So, horse, we ride; that is to say we move. Your head is in the air, you pick your feet off the ground. No longer the nag of Tevya the Drayman, but the horse of Tevya the Dairyman. Aye, people. Formerly when I was a pauper—that is to say two

13

weeks ago—everyone wished me well. Now they see me milking my two skinny cows, they haven't got a decent word to say. Where did Tevya get them? He stole them; he's making illegal schnapps on the side. Will you ever get a word of praise from your own kind? It's admitted I make the best butter you can buy. Do you think a single Jewish customer would ever say so? Never. On the other hand, only yesterday the rich gentile banker from the North tasted my Golde's cheese. Do you know what he said? Tevel, says he, you serve a decent product even if you are only a dog of a Jew. Where can you get such praise from your own? (*He pulls the reins of the horse.*) No. No more deliveries today. Today we're seeing Lazar Wolf, the Butcher. I'm opposed to the whole idea, but when Golde makes up her mind to something— it's done. Go see the butcher, she says. He's anxious to speak to you. Why, I answer; he's already got an eye on our little milch cow? Never mind, she tells me; you'll see him. If he offers a good price, you'll sell her—she's not such a great milker. No, I reply. It's written —— She interrupts the quotation and tells me Every Thursday when our Tzeitl is in his shop he tells her Send your papa to my house. I want to see him. I say No. She says Tevya! I repeat the No and here I am. As the Midrash tells us, Man proposes but who makes up his mind for him—Golde. (*Tevya leaves the wagon and enters Lazar Wolf's at R. The Butcher's is a substantial dwelling for a Russian Jew. The furniture is solid. Tevya wanders about, alone, looking, touching, testing, peeking. Calling aloud.*) Lazar Wolf—you're here? You're not here?—It's me, Tevya.

LAZAR. (*Off.*) I'll be right there. Make yourself at home, Reb Tevya.

TEVYA. "Make yourself at home." All right. It is a home. In my house you sit on a chair so. (*Sits on the edge.*) Here. (*Sits solidly.*) That's a chair. (*Examines the table. Bangs it.*) Mine would have come down with such a blow. (*Sees a samovar.*) A brass samovar. A butcher, as is written, is a man of substance. What I wouldn't give to see my daughters the mistress of such a house. (*Sees a goblet near the samovar.*) Mmm, a fine cup to drink from. A cup? A goblet! To make a toast with. Nu. L'chaim. (*Pretends to drain it. Lazar Wolf stomps in: a big man, drying beefy hands on a white, stained apron.*)

LAZAR. L'chaim to you, Rebb Tevya. You like it? It's yours. A present.

TEVYA. I couldn't.

LAZAR. What do you mean you couldn't? Do it; it's done. I'm sorry you had to wait. I was just butchering an ox.

TEVYA. (*Puts cup down.*) It's no good, Lazar Wolf, I won't do it. Golde insisted I come, so I came; but the answer is No.

LAZAR. Sit down, take a glass of tea, let's talk like sensible people. First listen, then say No.

TEVYA. I'll listen but No is no.

LAZAR. Let's begin at the beginning. How are things with you? (*Hands Tevya the tea.*)

TEVYA. (*Back to normal.*) How are things? I go and I go and I go and I get nowhere. As the Torah says Money is round—it rolls away.

LAZAR. Yes, but compared to the way things were ——

TEVYA. You heard?

LAZAR. Of course, I heard. A butcher hears about things.

TEVYA. I told you No.

LAZAR. All right, No. But let's talk. A piece of hard sugar?

TEVYA. Thank you.

LAZAR. Compared to yesterday, Reb Tevya, you're a rich man ——

TEVYA. As the Talmud says: May we both have what I still need to make me a rich man.

LAZAR. It's a wonderful thing to be a learned man, Reb Tevya, and have a line of Talmud for every occasion ——

TEVYA. There's a quotation for that too, Lazar Wolf.

LAZAR. I'm sure, I'm sure —— However, business is business, so let's begin ——

TEVYA. You heard my answer already.

LAZAR. Listen, give a man a chance.

TEVYA. There's no sense in wasting your breath. A No from Tevya means No.

LAZAR. Why not?

TEVYA. I'm in no hurry. My house isn't on fire—and besides, I feel sorry for the poor thing.

LAZAR. Listen to him, he feels sorry. You talk as if she's the only one you've got.

TEVYA. She's my first—there's none like her.

LAZAR. I know, I know how you feel. Everyone is special—

15

each one. But we are men of the world. There'd be a little something in it, for you—Lazar Wolf is not a stingy man.

TEVYA. I heard last year, in the dead of winter, you gave away ice.

LAZAR. Maybe I'm a little rough in business. But this is a family matter.

TEVYA. What are you talking about—*a family matter*—what family?

LAZAR. Wait a minute, Tevya, what have you been talking about?

TEVYA. My cow, what else?

LAZAR. (*Laughing.*) His cow, that's a great one.

TEVYA. So what are *you* talking about? Tell me, please, so I can laugh, too. Tevya also enjoys a joke.

LAZAR. I'm talking about your *daughter*, what else? Tzeitl—your eldest.

TEVYA. You want my Tzeitl? No. Impossible. Absolutely no. No, and again No.

LAZAR. I gather you don't like the idea, why?

TEVYA. Why, he asks. You're a butcher.

LAZAR. A butcher always has meat in the house.

TEVYA. You're an old man, twice her age.

LAZAR. I'm not older than you are, and you're a young man.

TEVYA. You're a widower with grown children.

LAZAR. My children are married and a widower has the experience of a mature man.

TEVYA. Nah—you haven't the right kind of feelings for a delicate girl like Tzeitl. Her singing, her sewing, her cooking—could you appreciate her subtleties?

LAZAR. When it comes to eating, Lazar Wolf is not backward.

TEVYA. No, no and again No!

LAZAR. Now let me talk. (*Tevya turns his back.*) I'm pretty well off, Reb Tevya. I have, heaven will forgive my boasting, my own house. Try the table.

TEVYA. I tried.

LAZAR. I have two shops: here and in Boiberik. In my attic there are hides—in my chest, a little money.

TEVYA. Money is not everything.

LAZAR. If, worse luck, your Tzeitl found herself a man of solid substance, a good provider, with a mature head on his shoulders

16

and a Sabbath chicken for her father every week—plus no dowry and a little something for all the other daughters as well—is that a calamity?

TEVYA. ————.

LAZAR. Why are you silent?

TEVYA. I'm thinking. And thoughts are private, if you don't mind. I'm thinking, as it says in Rashi, from the heart. Good looking you're not—still good looks is on the surface.

LAZAR. Exactly.

TEVYA. Further, you're not a scholar. You can just about manage to say your prayers. But after all everybody can't be a scholar and Tevya can quote for two, at least. As the saying goes, If it's your luck to have a little money, well, there's learning in a bank account. But I'm still thinking No.

LAZAR. We don't have to bargain with each other, Reb Tevya, and beat around the bush. Let's shake hands and call it a match, what do you say? Speak up ——

TEVYA. What do you want me to do: yell? This is not something a person drives into—like a wagon—this is my oldest daughter ——

LAZAR. Exactly. Once she's out of the way you'll have a chance to concentrate on your second oldest and your third ——

TEVYA. To marry a daughter is no trick. When God, at His own pace, decides to send for each child her predestined one ——

LAZAR. Naturally, but does it hurt, Reb Tevya, to help our destiny a little? This one you can get rid of without a dowry. That'll leave a little something for the second one. Clothes, I told you I'd take care of, and if you yourself would consider something ——

TEVYA. A daughter is not a piece of meat to bargain over. You think you're still in the butcher store ——

LAZAR. I'm sorry if I offended. I'll say no more. Only where is it written that Lazar Wolf is not destined to be her predestined one?

TEVYA. That's a sensible answer. If it's meant to be that my Tzeitl will have a nice and comfortable life with Lazar Wolf, the butcher, with meat each day in the week ——

LAZAR. Every day.

TEVYA. Then it's written. But remember it's also written that a

17

woman is not a dishrag. Therefore Golde must be consulted, also the girl herself.

LAZAR. Of course, give them the pros and cons—I know your Golde is a practical woman —— Meanwhile, take the goblet I gave you—and have a drink ——

TEVYA. Well, why not? As the saying goes—a drink is a —— Not so much.

LAZAR. A real l'chaim this time.

TEVYA. Maybe a mazeltov.

LAZAR. Drink hearty.

TEVYA. (*Drinks.*) Do you know what a treasure she is?

LAZAR. I know.

TEVYA. A jewel—a pearl—a diamond.

LAZAR. What she'll eat in my house on week-days, she never eats in your house on holidays. Another?

TEVYA. (*Takes it.*) Don't think feeding a woman is everything. You can't eat five ruble pieces, and frankly, Reb Lazar Wolf— (That's nice schnapps)—you're a coarse fellow, something of a bull yourself ——

LAZAR. Agreed. Everything is agreed.

TEVYA. If you had a million rubles on one side of the scales and my Tzeitl on the other ——

LAZAR. Believe me, my father-in-law-to-be, I understand. Even if you are older than I am, Tevya, you're a bigger fool—I understand —— (*In great, good humor, they embrace, as the scene fades. CROSS FADE. Tevya weaves his way home. A little drunk, singing a Rosh Hashona song suggestive of the forthcoming wedding. He carries the goblet before him. Then realizes where he is—home—and enters cautiously. Lights on revealing Golde waiting for him. Face to face.*)

GOLDE. Oh, that's a shining example for a father of seven girls to come home drunk!

TEVYA. Golde, if I'm a little happy, believe me I have cause. Behold—a silver goblet.

GOLDE. I know all about it. Quick, go put cold water on your face—there's a thousand things to do. I've already got the pencil and paper.

TEVYA. What are you talking about? I only just walked in the door. I haven't even told you the good news and ——

GOLDE. I know. I know.

TEVYA. What do you know?

GOLDE. Tzeitl is engaged. To Lazar Wolf. I know. Without a dowry. I know. He'll buy the clothes. I know everything.

TEVYA. (Drying his face.) How do you know?

GOLDE. If you think a butcher hears about a cow quickly, let me tell you a mother hears about the engagement of her daughter before that. Besides, my Tevya, from Lazar Wolf's you staggered to the rabbi's house about the marriage contract. Then you managed to arrive at your wagon and there stood Pessie, the wife of the Cantor and Pessie has a tongue from here to Yehupetz. Besides, I knew it even before you left.

TEVYA. What?!

GOLDE. My Grandmother Tzeitl, may she rest in peace, for whom our Tzeitl is named, came to me in a vision, a dream. She stood in the doorway, holding by her hand our Tzeitl, and she was dressed as a bride.

TEVYA. Grandma Tzeitl was dressed as a bride ——!?

GOLDE. Our Tzeitl was the bride. Grandma was dressed in her Sabbath best, the blue dress and with the grey shawl over her head, that Papa gave her on their 15th anniversary. She led our Tzeitl into the room. And there standing under the canopy was the Rabbi, waiting to start the ceremony.

TEVYA. And the bridegroom?

GOLDE. To tell you the truth I didn't get a good look at his face. But now I realize it was Lazar Wolf. So sit down, there's a million things to do. Take the pencil ——

TEVYA. It is written that a woman is like a melon. Who knows what's inside?

GOLDE. For one night spare me the quotations and listen what you have to tell Lazar Wolf our Tzeitl needs. First of all she doesn't have a thing to wear, not a pair of stockings. She'll need a silk dress for the wedding—blue is her best color —— Write ——

TEVYA. Blue ——

GOLDE. A cotton dress for summer; a wool dress for winter. Three petticoats, three shawls. Then there's handkerchiefs, a silk parasol, night gowns and at least two pairs of other things . . .

TEVYA. You're going too fast. Other things? What's that?

GOLDE. Just put it down. Other things. Two pairs.

19

TEVYA. (*Writing.*) Tell me, my darling, where did you become acquainted with all this paraphernalia for fancy ladies?

GOLDE. I'm not a lady of fashion? I'm not used to silks and satins? Besides, I haven't got eyes when a train comes through? Listen, give *me* the list, I'll take it to Lazar Wolf myself—you wouldn't even know how to *pronounce* half of them ——

TEVYA. (*Thinking the whole thing over. Pleased.*) We made a good match, Golde.

GOLDE. Our Tzeitl will be a happy girl.

TEVYA. We thank Thee, Heavenly Father, that Thou has moved Lazar Wolf to take our daughter Tzeitl, without even a dowry. May she grow old with him in contentment and honor, not like Fruma-Sarah, his first wife, may *she* rest in peace. May we know the joy of seeing her the mistress of a fine house, filled to overflowing—in the backyard, chicken coops and goose coops and duck coops. Amen.

GOLDE. (*Affectionately.*) Sometimes, Tevya, you are not such a fool. Amen.

TEVYA. Now—where's the bride-to-be? TZEITL! Tzeitl! (*The three girls walk through stiffly from* L. *Tzeitl is crying.*) She's crying for joy. (*To Tzeitl.*) You heard.

TZEITL. (*Crying.*) Papa ——

HODEL. Tzeitl, we agreed. (*And the three girls stand stonily in silence.*)

TEVYA. What's the matter?

TZEITL. (*Running off* R.) Oh, papa, I ——

TEVYA. Go with her. Find out. (*Golde leaves* R. *To Hodel.*) What's the matter with your sister? I did something, Hodel?

HODEL. Look at me, papa.

TEVYA. (*He looks.*) I see. I committed a crime. What crime?

HODEL. Did it ever occur to you that Tzeitl has some feelings in the matter?

TEVYA. It occurred to me that Tzeitl likes to eat every day.

HODEL. What does she want, papa—that's the important question.

TEVYA. Why, she doesn't want to be warm winter as well as summer?

HODEL. Did the question ever come into your mind—does she love this man?

20

TEVYA. The novels of Paris and St. Petersburg are with us. Waltzes is not something to live on, my darling.

HODEL. You're not listening to what I'm saying.

TEVYA. Give me a quotation, maybe then I'll understand.

HODEL. Your head is so full of quotations, you don't see what's going on under your nose.

TEVYA. Enlighten your papa. He's listening.

HODEL. The world is changing, papa. People are changing. Tzeitl has a right to her own life.

TEVYA. *Rights*, this is what you're talking about?

HODEL. Today is not yesterday, papa.

TEVYA. Now it's clear to me. Yesterday they ate bread; today they chew on rights.

HODEL. You don't marry off a daughter. You ask a daughter.

TEVYA. This I intended all along. I said it even to Lazar Wolf. The girl herself, I said, is not a dishrag. Ask him if I didn't say that.

HODEL. (*Walks to the table and picks up the goblet.*) You made your arrangements. You had a drink on it. You signed a marriage contract. You set a date with the rabbi. Did you or didn't you?

TEVYA. I did. Sentence me to prison for life. Only put down the goblet before you break it.

HODEL. You think because a thing has been done for a thousand years, it has to be that way forever. Talk to Tzeitl. Listen to her. With both your ears. Go, papa. Ask her.

TEVYA. The mother takes the words out of your mouth before you get a chance to speak. The daughter puts new ones in before you can draw a second breath. It is written truly ——

HODEL. Papa!

TEVYA. I'm going. (*He starts walking. To no one in particular.*) Modern children. (*Tevya joins Golde and Tzeitl stage* R. *This is the wagon shed.*) So, my Tzeitl, come to your papa's arms and tell me. (*He takes Tzeitl from Golde's arms and as he embraces her, speaks to Golde over her shoulder. Sotto.*) What is it?

GOLDE. (*Same.*) Tears. All I hear is tears. No and tears.

TEVYA. I'll talk to her. I'm the father.

GOLDE. Talk, but don't say too much. Don't say anything you'll be sorry for.

TEVYA. Tevya the Dairyman doesn't talk out of both sides of his mouth.

GOLDE. (*Going.*) Lazar Wolf's don't grow on trees.

TEVYA. So, my biggest girl, my silliest, biggest girl, tell me.

TZEITL. Papa, I'm so unhappy.

TEVYA. Why? Your father is asking why.

TZEITL. I don't want to marry him.

TEVYA. And the reason?

TZEITL. I don't love him, papa.

TEVYA. Love, I'll tell you about. Love doesn't always happen in the morning. Sometimes it takes all afternoon and part of the evening.

TZEITL. I'll carry stones. I'll dig holes. I'll be a servant for the gentiles.

TEVYA. What terrible life am I sending you to? I'm rescuing you. No more three in a bed. No more without supper. Look at the dress you're wearing.

TZEITL. I couldn't, papa. Never.

TEVYA. You enjoy it so much being the daughter in a house where the wind runs through everything?

TZEITL. How can I tell you? I'd be fed and warm—but in that house, papa, I would die.

TEVYA. So much you don't want to?

TZEITL. Please, papa, have pity on me.

TEVYA. Tevya's daughters will never be unhappy. Hungry maybe; but never unhappy. You don't want to marry him, that's all there is to it. After all, today is not yesterday.

TZEITL. Thank you, papa.

TEVYA. Not me; the Lord in Heaven, who opened my eyes. Did you think I was going to force you? Never. Even if in some circles a rich man is not a calamity.

TZEITL. Papa, you're wonderful.

TEVYA. Listen, what Tevya thought was preordained was not ordained. So be it. Done and done. Wipe your eyes; you've done enough crying for one day. (*He blows her nose.*) So—I'll return his goblet in the morning. I'll make my explanations to the rabbi. As the Good Book tells us. Period.

TZEITL. Papa, could I talk to you?

TEVYA. Something else?

TZEITL. I think this is the best time. (*Calling offstage.*) Psst. It's all right. Come out.

TEVYA. What's going on? (*Enter Mottel. He is a small thread-bare but ingratiating, young tailor.*)

TZEITL. Papa, you know Mottel Kamzoil.

TEVYA. The tailor from Anatevka—what brings you here?

MOTTEL. I walked, Reb Tevya.

TEVYA. That I didn't ask you. What I asked was what is Mottel Kamzoil, all the way from Anatevka, doing in Tevya's barn?

MOTTEL. I came because I have a match for Tzeitl.

TEVYA. Since when did a tailor become a matchmaker? Is it a good match?

MOTTEL. Like a glove fits a hand.

TEVYA. In whose behalf are you here? If he smells from a butcher shop—no!

MOTTEL. This is a match that was made—as we say in the shop —to the measure.

TEVYA. Who, please?

MOTTEL. Who else?—We love each other.

TZEITL. We gave each other our pledge over a year ago ——

TEVYA. You gave yourself your pledge? And where was I? What about my rights—or is this also part of today that a father is treated like dust?

MOTTEL. Nothing like that, Reb Tevya. I've been working in the shop, to get a little ahead, so that when I came to ask you I would have a little something to start in life with ——

TEVYA. What's the matter—a father doesn't give a dowry any more?

MOTTEL. Up until just recently, Reb Tevya, no offense meant, you weren't exactly in a position to ——

TEVYA. That's not the point. Now let me ask some questions: a father asks questions. How do you expect to support my Tzeitl, a tailor with one shirt to his name?

MOTTEL. When you married your Golde, did you have a large mansion?

TEVYA. All right—passed. What kind of a family do you come from?

MOTTEL. My family is my family. I have a trade. That no one can take from me. The name I haven't made yet.

TEVYA. You know something: that's a good answer. My own pedigree isn't exactly aristocratic, so why am I giving myself airs?

TZEITL. Oh, papa, papa ——

TEVYA. Still to deny to an old man the pleasure of his rights?—
"to go and pledge"—such a word—without giving a father the
joy of a drink and a mazeltov and a little arguing back and
forth ——

MOTTEL. We're having it right now—Reb Tevya, aren't we?

TEVYA. Maybe he is only a tailor, but he's a good man. He'll
make a living by the sweat of his brow—like your father. So let's
give thanks to God —— You won't change your mind tomorrow?

MOTTEL. May I become a stone, a bone—and sink into earth
right here if I ever change my mind.

TEVYA. Tzeitl?

TZEITL. I love him, papa.

TEVYA. Thy will be done. We thank Thee, O Heavenly Father,
who in His infinite wisdom has sent forth Mottel, the Tailor, for
Tzeitl, the daughter of Tevya, the daughter of Golde —— (*He
stops.*) Your mama! What will I tell your mama?

MOTTEL. We'll tell her ourselves, Reb Tevya.

TZEITL. You've done enough already, papa.

TEVYA. No. And when Tevya says No regarding Golde, it's No.

TZEITL. What will you tell her?

TEVYA. The truth. The truth, as is written, can be stated in several ways. If a little something is left out—it can still be the truth.
Or if a drop is added that doesn't make it a lie. Like the time the
Czar's general came to my father to take me into the Army. My
father replied the boy is crazy, your honor; look in his eyes; he
wouldn't make a good soldier. Crazy, I wasn't; but a good soldier
I wouldn't have been. My father helped the Czar. Right? So go,
my children, and be happy. The problem of Golde is between
Tevya and his Maker. (*LIGHTS FADE SLOWLY OUT. When
they come up again, Golde and Tevya are both asleep in the bed
u. L. Tevya sits bolt upright. Feigning talking in his sleep.*) No.
Help! Stop. No!

GOLDE. (*Awakening.*) Tevya! I'm next to you. Wake up. What
is it?

TEVYA. She's here. She's there. She's gone. She's back. She's on
top of me!

GOLDE. Wake up, Tevya, you're raving.

TEVYA. Help. Quick! Lights, water! She's choking me. Help!

(*The LIGHTS go on, as Hodel and Tzeitl enter* L. *carrying candles.*)

GOLDE. It's a dream. A glass of water for papa. Quick. (*Tzeitl goes for the water.*)

TEVYA. Where am I?

GOLDE. You had a dream. Arise, blink your eyes, spit three times and turn from the moon. (*Tevya drinks.*)

TEVYA. She's there. I can still see her! Don't you see her?

GOLDE. There's nobody there, Tevya. Back to bed, girls. Your papa'll be all right.

TEVYA. Look! There. Your Grandmother Tzeitl for whom our Tzeitl is named. There!

GOLDE. My Grandmother Tzeitl, may she rest in peace, is not here, Tevya. It's only a dream. Girls, please. (*The girls withdraw* L., *but peek in. Tevya gets out of bed, Golde following.*)

TEVYA. Clearer than life I saw her, with her arm outstretched and speaking so loud it was like thunder. Then she grabbed me by the windpipe and began choking the life out of me.

GOLDE. My Grandmother Tzeitl?!

TEVYA. No, Fruma-Sarah, Lazar Wolf's first wife ——

GOLDE. Grandmother Tzeitl and Fruma-Sarah in one dream; *that's* a nightmare! Tell it slowly from the beginning.

TEVYA. You remember your dream about Grandmother Tzeitl and the wedding of our Tzeitl, with the Rabbi there and the canopy and all the guests ——?

GOLDE. Don't tell me my dream; tell me your dream.

TEVYA. It was the same as yours, except Grandma Tzeitl came toward me, holding her arm out toward the wedding canopy. Congratulations, she says, you made a wise choice ——

GOLDE. What was she wearing?

TEVYA. I didn't look.

GOLDE. You didn't see what she had on for a wedding?

TEVYA. Oh, of course, I saw. A shroud. All in white she was. Like a tomb.

GOLDE. She came to a wedding in a shroud?

TEVYA. Maybe she had on a shawl over the shroud? I think so. Yes, the one you said ——

GOLDE. The grey one Papa gave her on their anniversary?

TEVYA. That's the one.

GOLDE. Of course. My grandmother would never come to a wedding in a shroud.

TEVYA. So she came toward me and said You made a wise choice.

GOLDE. Naturally, Grandma knew Lazar Wolf.

TEVYA. No, listen. Her exact words were as follows: My children, she said, Mottel Kamzoil will make her a fine husband.

GOLDE. The tailor! What's the tailor doing under the canopy in your dream with our Tzeitl? It's Lazar Wolf!

TEVYA. Listen, your grandmother says, Mottel Kamzoil is named for Uncle Mordecai. It's a sign he'll make Tzeitl a good husband.

GOLDE. You didn't hear her right ——

TEVYA. Please stop interrupting my nightmare. They'll grow old together, she says. Even if he is only a tailor with one shirt to his name. God willing, she says, they'll be happy together. Then, like a puff of smoke, suddenly she's standing next to me—with one finger outstretched, accusing, like I robbed her.

GOLDE. *My* grandmother wouldn't be in a puff of smoke!

TEVYA. You're not listening. It wasn't your grandmother in the smoke. It was Fruma-Sarah, Lazar's wife. And, oh, the face on her. Yellow, she was, like wax. Right away, as in life, she opens her mouth and out it pours. If your daughter Tzeitl marries my Lazar Wolf, and wears my clothes and opens my closets then I feel sorry for her and sorry for you and sorry for your wife as well. (Although, she adds, in life your wife and I didn't have two good words to exchange in a year.)

GOLDE. She spoke true.

TEVYA. (*Driving right on.*) Rich she'll be, says Fruma-Sarah. Fed she'll be, your Tzeitl, but not for long. If she marries my Lazar, when three weeks are over, I'll come in the night. And she grabs me by the windpipe and begins choking. It's a wonder I'm alive.

GOLDE. Spit three times, again. It's an evil spirit. May it sink in the earth, may it drown in the river, may it lose itself in the forest and be gone into the sky. Ptui, ptui, ptui.

TEVYA. Then Fruma-Sarah disappeared and your Grandmother Tzeitl took our Tzeitl by the arm and led her to the canopy where Mottel Kamzoil is waiting and the wedding began ——

GOLDE. It's a sign from heaven and from the other place. Mottel Kamzoil is worth more than Lazar Wolf, even if he is only a Tailor. His little finger is better than the butcher's whole body. And, after all, since he's named for my Uncle Mordecai, he couldn't be a tailor by birth. It's a temporary situation. Like the time my grandfather (may he rest in peace) was unemployed for fourteen years.

TEVYA. It's a wonder I'm alive.

GOLDE. You'll have to go quick and see Mottel Kamzoil and have a talk.

TEVYA. I'll do that.

GOLDE. And we'll talk to Tzeitl.

TEVYA. First thing in the morning. (*They get back to bed.*)

GOLDE. Oh, I come from a fine family, Tevya. Did you ever know such a thoughtful person as my Grandmother Tzeitl? To come all the way back from the true world of Paradise to worry about one of my seven.

TEVYA. Did she have to frighten the life out of me?

GOLDE. It was an emergency. All right, back to bed. Put a little cotton in your ears to keep out the Evil One. Girls, you're still up? Lights out and good night.

TZEITL. (*Entering* L.) Good night, Mama. Good night, Papa. (*She kisses him.*) I love you very much. (*Hodel kisses him. The girls go. AS LIGHTS FADE.*)

TEVYA. (*Things have settled down. He looks heavenward.*) It's written that each man has his affliction. Meaning Tevya is a little bit of a liar. (*THE LIGHTS FADE OUT.*)

CURTAIN

ACT II

HODEL

Tevya is driving his horse home. The mood is relaxed. He has had a good day. The time is toward twilight.

TEVYA. Well, horse, we had a good day. We sold everything down to the last crumb of cheese. Listen how the empty cans rattle. Music. Therefore, as is written, Give thanks and lift your voice in praise. I'll sing. (*He hums a strain or two, stops.*) No. The sages also tell us Preserve the community in Israel. Wound not, they write, the feelings of thy fellow men; strive always to be at one with them. Therefore, I'll put on a long face and plod along beside you. Why, you ask. I'll explain. Suppose I pass a friend in the road and he asks Tevya, how did you make out today? I answer Terrible; I lost everything! never was there such a black day. Then he's happy with what I told him; I was happy already. We're both happy. You see? Maintain the community in Israel. In this fashion the delicate feelings of my fellow men are preserved. In the study of the Torah all things are possible. (*Confidentially to the horse.*) But, now, since we're alone—Halleluyah, praise God and a happy day! Wait, what's in the road? (*He peers ahead.*) Robbers? No. Besides, why am I afraid of robbers? The last robbers brought Tevya his fortune. Nah—this is a lone wanderer. Also a skinny one. Nothing to worry about—a schlimazl. Whoa. (*To Feferal.*) You're going this way? (*Feferal appears on the road from R. He is a thin, wiry student, dressed in rags and carrying a bundle of books. A bright, bird-like man, thin as a toothpick, he is about twenty-one.*)

FEFERAL. I'm trying to.

TEVYA. So climb in. I have plenty of room.

FEFERAL. That's very good of you. Thank you. (*Feferal takes his place in the wagon beside Tevya and during the rest of the scene they drive home.*)

TEVYA. Apparently, my young friend, you are not acquainted with the teachings of the Fathers. (This milk can is the softest.) It is written If thou seest the ass of your enemy fallen under its burden, thou shall not pass it by. Meaning, extend the same courtesy to a human being that you would to a ——

FEFERAL. (*Laughing.*) It's too bad more people don't practice what they preach as you do, Reb Tevya.

TEVYA. Oh, you know me. So if you know who I am, who are you?

FEFERAL. I'm a man.

TEVYA. That I know. Four feet you haven't got, therefore, you are not a horse. But, as we Jews say, whose are you?

FEFERAL. As we Jews answer—whose should I be but God's?

TEVYA. That, too, I know, since all living things are His. But from whom are you descended? Who is your father?

FEFERAL. My father is your father: Adam, from whom all men are descended.

TEVYA. A tongue on wheels, I see. My friend, are you from around here or are you possibly from Lithuania?

FEFERAL. And if I were from Lithuania?

TEVYA. It's just an expression; some are Jews, some are from Lithuania.

FEFERAL. A joke is funny, Reb Tevya, but to poke fun of people ——

TEVYA. *Are* you from Lithuania?

FEFERAL. No.

TEVYA. So why all the fuss?

FEFERAL. It's a matter of principle with me, Reb Tevya.

TEVYA. It's a matter of principle with me that a man who knows my name, I also should know his name. Now tell me who is your father.

FEFERAL. The question of who ——

TEVYA. (*Overriding.*) Look, my boy, Tevya likes a disputation too; but once in a while, give a person a straight answer. Who is the father who begat you? Am I clear? Who, when you need it, do you turn to and say, Papa, I need a ruble?

FEFERAL. (*Laughs.*) You know my father very well, Reb Tevya. His name is Perchick.

TEVYA. Perchick, the cigarette maker? Then you must be Feferal, son of Perchick.

FEFERAL. That's who I am.

TEVYA. Ah, Perchick. How is your papa?

FEFERAL. He works from sunrise to sunset. The price of tobacco is up. At the end of a week he has enough left over to make one cigarette from himself.

TEVYA. I see, business as usual; that's nice to know. So where have you been keeping yourself? We haven't seen you in a long time.

FEFERAL. I've been studying in Yehupetz.

TEVYA. A student gentleman. And what would the young gentleman be studying in Yehupetz?

FEFERAL. The young gentleman is preparing for his examinations for the University.

TEVYA. Why?

FEFERAL. To improve myself.

TEVYA. Improve is a good word. Study the Torah.

FEFERAL. Yes, the Torah, too, is a fine book.

TEVYA. Too? In the Torah, my friend, you're on Tevya's home grounds. The Five Books of Moses is ——

FEFERAL. The Torah is not the only book of wisdom, Reb Tevya.

TEVYA. Let Tevya finish one sentence, please. In the Torah there is a question: How will the generations live while they are at school studying? Answer that.

FEFERAL. We live on what we eat.

TEVYA. A good answer—and what do you eat?

FEFERAL. I eat whatever I can get.

TEVYA. You hear it, horse; this younger generation. Sons of cobblers and cigarette makers, off they go to the cities to become scholars. They sleep in garrets; they starve. And why—to improve themselves. Now a serious question. Tell me why all this study, since when all is said and done and you've digested all the fine print, the only sign you can read says: Keep Off the Grass?

FEFERAL. That's the Czar's idea. The Little Father has lots of ideas like that. But *our* idea is to change it.

TEVYA. Aha! Change it.

FEFERAL. When all the poor get together, Reb Tevya ——

TEVYA. I know all about it. The bottom rail becomes the top rail and if my Grandmother Nechama, may she rest in peace, had wings, she'd be a bird ——

FEFERAL. You don't even begin to understand.

TEVYA. Tevya the Dairyman understands. Every morning he serves them in their summer houses and soft beds. The rich.

FEFERAL. Don't talk to me about the rich. They're no friends of mine. It's the poor who count ——

TEVYA. I know. In your opinion poverty is a gift of God. Listen, sonny, work is noble, but money is comfortable.

FEFERAL. Money is a curse.

TEVYA. May Tevya be so cursed and never recover.

FEFERAL. You have a lot to learn, even if you are an old man——

TEVYA. You're not shy. I'll say that for you, even if you're thin as a matchstick and less than nothing to look at. But, tell me: did the rich perhaps steal away your father's inheritance and divide it among themselves?

FEFERAL. It may well be that all of us shall have no small share in their inheritance and sooner than you think.

TEVYA. From your mouth, sonny, into God's ears. May it come to pass that all of us have enough to eat and some to spare. Meanwhile, I'll give you a parable about don't break your head on a stone wall.

FEFERAL. What seems impossible to you ——

TEVYA. Let a man your father's age speak a parable, then answer. Yerechmoil Moses, the Hebrew Teacher, is blind in one eye and nearsighted in the other. On his nose he wears a pair of spectacles. The lens on one side is broken, on the other side there is no lens. You ask him why he wears them, he'll tell you. It's better than nothing, isn't it?

FEFERAL. Your world is bounded on the East by Anatevka, Reb Tevya, and on the west by Boiberik. You don't know what's going on today. There is something new in the air. The world is quivering with change and preparations and ——

TEVYA. (Stands in the wagon.) Wait and whoa and stop. Horse and Feferal Perchick. Take a deep breath. (He inhales expansively.) The air is quivering. True. With Golde's blintzes and Golde's borscht. Inhale. I'm home.

FEFERAL. I like you, Reb Tevya.

TEVYA. I also like you. Your ideas I wouldn't give you a kopeck for. Let your enemies have such ideas. But you're a person who can chase an argument up and down a flight of stairs. And this Tevya enjoys more than a glass of tea. So when can you come and visit and conclude the disputation?

FEFERAL. I could come right now.

TEVYA. You're certainly not bashful. The smell, hmmm? One thing I'm sure of. You'll find my Golde's cooking and my daughters' company more to your taste than my arguments. (*The two enter the house as the LIGHTS FADE OUT. Tevya's house, several weeks later. Tevya, Feferal and Hodel are at the kitchen table, talking. Feferal has been eating, Tevya has a glass of tea. Golde serves and clears. The little ones listen, enjoying the excitement and the company.*)

FEFERAL. (*His fork poised in the air.*) What I've been trying to get through your head for the last two weeks is that the world will be different ——

TEVYA. I heard you for the last two weeks. In your world there will be no more wars, no poverty, no hatred; no czars, no czarinas, no czarovitches ——

FEFERAL. He heard me!

TEVYA. Also no Turks, no Russians, no Jews, only people—all friends.

FEFERAL. Now you're beginning to understand ——

TEVYA. On that day the trumpet will sound the Messiah will be standing outside Tevya's house—in person.

FEFERAL. No, no. It's not a dream.

TEVYA. (*Amazed at such apostasy.*) Who said a dream? The Messiah is not a dream. Some day. But it may take Tevya's lifetime, your lifetime, and a little beyond ——

FEFERAL. A great man said If we will it, it can be done.

TEVYA. You're quoting? In the Midrash is a proper quotation. It happens, says the Midrash that even the honest may succceed—but rarely.

FEFERAL. Reb Tevya, Reb Tevya, you listen but you don't listen.

TEVYA. You're talking changes? Tevya will tell you changes. First, fix the roof on the synagogue in Anatevka, so on the High Holidays, in the rain, it doesn't leak.

HODEL. Oh, papa!

TEVYA. Second, we need a new bathhouse. The old one, the walls will surely cave in one day while the women are bathing.

HODEL. Papa, Feferal isn't talking about walls that need fixing.

TEVYA. What Feferal is talking about Feferal can say himself. With a tongue like his, help he doesn't need. Now I lost my place ——

CHAVA. You fixed the bathhouse, Papa.

TEVYA. (*Eyeing her.*) Thank you. (*Back to the discussion now.*) Third, a hospital, such a hospital it'll be a pleasure to get sick. And, last, get rid of Yankel Sheigetz as President of the Burial Society. (There's been too much swindling at the funerals.) Now there's a program for you—changes.

FEFERAL. (*Gesturing again with his fork.*) All right, your bathhouse, your synagogue, your hospital—how do you think you get such things, out of thin air?

GOLDE. Look at him. His fork is in the air. He's reforming the world and the potato pancakes under his nose are getting cold.

HODEL. Oh, mama—not now!

GOLDE. Is it true?

FEFERAL. It's true.

GOLDE. So, take a hot one; put the fork in your mouth, get a little fat on your bones. You'll argue better also.

FEFERAL. (*Putting his fork down, in protest.*) I couldn't eat another thing. You take such good care of me I'm embarrassed.

GOLDE. Don't be embarrassed. Eat, eat. Look how you look.

FEFERAL. Honestly, I can't take another bite.

GOLDE. You don't like the pancakes?

FEFERAL. I like them very much. I've just had enough.

GOLDE. Too much salt?

FEFERAL. No, no.

GOLDE. Not enough salt?

FEFERAL. The salt is fine. Believe me.

GOLDE. So take another one. (*She plunks down another potato pancake.*)

TEVYA. If a person doesn't stuff himself till he can't move, he doesn't like your cooking. Leave the boy alone, he's not bashful.

GOLDE. It's the salt.

TEVYA. Two men are discussing the world, she's talking salt. (*Golde takes a pancake from the plate and tastes it. She leaves the table shaking her head: they taste fine to her.*)

HODEL. Papa, can we go on?

TEVYA. (*Facing Feferal.*) I'm listening.

HODEL. What you won't understand is that what you're talking about can't happen unless everything's changed from top to bottom ——

TEVYA. (*Turning to her, in surprise.*) Tell me, madam, since

33

when did the daughters of Tevya the Dairyman learn to swallow ideas like noodles?

FEFERAL. We've been doing a little talking, Reb Tevya. And reading. Hodel is a very bright girl.

TEVYA. Naturally. The apple falls not far from the tree. All right then—I'll ask you both a question. My two intellectuals. Your new world—(the one that's coming after the Sixth Millennium)—does this new world have a decent respect for matzos on Passover and for the Sabbath loaf on Friday night?

FEFERAL. It's not so simple, Reb Tevya ——

TEVYA. Wrong. Simple it is. Yes and no. Let me tell you, Feferal Perchick, a dispute on principle is fine. You want to rant against the Czar, I'm your man. But don't try to tell Tevya that anything good will not have a proper respect for the Talmud and the teachings of the Prophets.

HODEL. We didn't say that.

TEVYA. We. Now it's we? Listen, the both of you—we ——

HODEL. Let Feferal answer. Every time he opens his mouth, you jump in.

TEVYA. (*Toward Golde.*) Listen to your daughter.

CHAVA. It's true, Papa.

TEVYA. Now this one.

GOLDE. They're right. Every time you're listening, you're talking.

TEVYA. So, Tevya is silent. Is Tevya talking? I'm listening. Speak.

FEFERAL. (*Who has gotten out of his chair.*) What time is it?

TEVYA. Why? You have an appointment with the Prime Minister?

FEFERAL. I'm sorry, Reb Tevya, but I have to go.

TEVYA. Again?

FEFERAL. I know ——

TEVYA. This I don't like.

FEFERAL. I'm sorry, but I must ——

TEVYA. I like you. My wife and daughters like you. You're a comfort to an old man, like one of the family ——

FEFERAL. Thank you, I feel the same way.

TEVYA. But this business of getting up and disappearing. Which is getting to be a habit. This I don't like. Where are you running?

FEFERAL. I can't tell you.

TEVYA. The same answer. Two nights ago, I'm in the middle of a quotation from Elijah. Boom—out the door you vanished. Tonight the same thing. Why?

FEFERAL. I wish I could tell you.

TEVYA. Secrets. Did anything good ever come from secrets?

HODEL. Papa, it's healthier if you don't know.

TEVYA. And you know? For you it's healthy, for me it's un-healthy. Explain.

FEFERAL. I can't. I have to go. Good night, Chava, good night, Hodel.

CHAVA. Could I have the book? (*Chava refers to a book Hodel has been leafing. Feferal nods. Tevya turns to find out what new development is taking place when Golde crosses toward Feferal, attracting Tevya's attention.*)

GOLDE. Here.

FEFERAL. What is it?

GOLDE. (*Handing him the package.*) The pancakes you didn't eat. Eat them later.

FEFERAL. Oh, I couldn't.

GOLDE. I was right. Too much salt.

FEFERAL. No, they're wonderful. Of course, I'll take them. (*He takes the package.*)

GOLDE. It's a sin to let good food go to waste. (*Feferal joins Tevya and the two walk to the door—somewhat away from the others in the room.*)

FEFERAL. Reb Tevya, may I say something to you? This business of my having to leave and not explaining. If you don't want me to come back again, just say so.

TEVYA. Tevya's door is never closed to a friend. Only, sonny, you're not in with thieves?

FEFERAL. Believe me, my friends are the finest in the world ——

TEVYA. I take your word. Tevya is not an old woman who has to know everything. You couldn't give me a hint? (*Feferal laughs.*) Even so I like you. A man who sticks to his principles. Go. When you're finished, come again.

FEFERAL. Could I say something else?

TEVYA. Suddenly the Matchstick is shy.

FEFERAL. What I mean is—you have fine daughters, Reb Tevya.

TEVYA. Ohho. You notice things beside the great new world that's dawning!

FEFERAL. I just wanted to say it. We'll talk again, but I assure you that I have as much respect for true religion as any man on earth ——

TEVYA. (*Lightly teasing.*) But the Sabbath Loaf is not so simple ——

FEFERAL. Next time we'll talk until we finish the subject. I
promise. I'll bring a book ——

TEVYA. Don't bring a book. Bring yourself.

FEFERAL. As soon as I can. (*They shake hands warmly and
Feferal leaves.*)

TEVYA. Crazy as a bedbug. But a fine boy. His ideas —— (*To
Hodel.*) Stay away from his ideas. (*To Chava.*) You, too. My
enemies should have such ideas. Tell me, does he keep his mouth
shut outdoors at least?

HODEL. You said it yourself, Papa. He's a person of principle.
He's the kind of person when he says something he means it.

GOLDE. Enough principle, enough talk. Your papa and I would
like a little peace and quiet. We have a few things on our mind.
(*The girls leave. Golde brings Tevya a glass of tea.*)

TEVYA. What are you thinking?

GOLDE. Are you asking me a question, or do you want to make
a long speech?

TEVYA. I'm asking.

GOLDE. Then take the advice of a woman with two eyes in her
head and go see Ephraim.

TEVYA. Ephraim, the Match-Maker?

GOLDE. He was here with an offer for our Hodel. A perfect mate,
he has. Rich, handsome, with an estate and horses. A prince of a
man, he said. At least a duke.

TEVYA. He's royalty, I know. What's wrong with him?

GOLDE. Nothing. He's a bachelor, going on thirty-seven,
Ephraim said. Maybe forty, I'm not sure. But he has all his own
teeth.

TEVYA. Never mind his teeth. Why all of a sudden is the match-
maker in our house and I have to see him?

GOLDE. Why? Because Hodel is not getting any younger. And
if not this match then maybe another match ——

TEVYA. You mean—(*He gestures after Feferal.*) nahh.

GOLDE. You don't see what's going on under your own nose?

TEVYA. Ah, what are you talking about?

GOLDE. Take the cotton out of your ears, and open your eyes.

TEVYA. They don't know each other two weeks ——

GOLDE. It takes time?

TEVYA. I'm the one he comes to see. The discussions. Besides, the only thing that one has in his head is—(*He gestures The Millenium.*) that.

GOLDE. A father of seven, he hasn't got the sense of a boiled potato.

TEVYA. Impossible. Without consulting Tevya; never.

GOLDE. It happened before in history. Therefore you'll see Ephraim.

TEVYA. Don't spin my head around like a top. I know my daughter. I know my man. I rely on their honor. I'm at peace. (*A pause.*) There is, however, I just thought of it—a quotation in the Talmud concerning such men as Feferal Perchick. Respect such men, our sages tell us. Honor them; but keep an eye on them.

GOLDE. Now you make a little sense. (*She starts cleaning up the table.*) You'll see Ephraim?

TEVYA. I'll look into the duke. (*There is a SLOW FADE OUT. Tevya stands alone outside his house. It is a day later. He is debating a course of action. He turns first, naturally, to God.*) You know what you're doing, O Lord. I hope you do. Bless the coming marriage of my daughter Hodel to ——

GOLDE. (*Within, calling.*) Tevya, it's you? (*Tevya takes a deep breath, then walks into the house with a buoyancy acquired for the occasion.*)

TEVYA. Everybody gather. Quick. Golde, children. Light the samovar. Get the table cloth. A happy day! (*As everyone gathers around excited, curious. Ad lib. comments: Tell me. What, Papa?*)

GOLDE. What happened? The horse broke his leg?

TEVYA. (*Busy speaking to his younger children—and in the process avoiding Golde.*) Shprinze, run to your sister Tzeitl's. Tell them get dressed. Tell Mottel the Tailor to bring his fiddle. Beilke, run for the rabbi. The rest put on your Sabbath best.

GOLDE. A wedding. You mean it?

TEVYA. Our Hodel is a bride. Lay out the white dress. Chava, get paper for the marriage contract. Run, quick, make hurry, do. (*The girls scurry off on their missions.*)

GOLDE. You did it so fast, Tevya?

TEVYA. Naturally. It takes time? (*Chava has returned with paper and pencil.*)

GOLDE. (*In the time-honored tradition of tears at joy.*) My

Hodel a bride. My little girl becomes a woman. So tell me everything.

TEVYA. (*To Chava.*) Sit here. I'll speak; you'll write.

GOLDE. (*Herself, immediately.*) What are the terms?

TEVYA. The terms. Excellent. No dowry. He gives everything. We give only the bride.

GOLDE. He wasn't wrong, Ephraim. A prince of a man. A king.

TEVYA. Who?

GOLDE. Who? Her husband, who.

TEVYA. On the top of the paper, write the name of the bride. Hodel. Write.

GOLDE. So put in his name ——

TEVYA. (*Busying himself with Chava.*) First comes the blessing. Write: Blessed art Thou, O Lord—her husband is Perchick ——

GOLDE. What?

TEVYA. They're getting married.

GOLDE. My Hodel and Feferal Perchick!

TEVYA. You don't know how lucky we are.

GOLDE. My enemies should have such luck. He has less to his name than Mottel Kamzoil. He's a chicken that isn't hatched yet. And that mouth of his ——

TEVYA. You don't know him. From the beginning there were signs.

GOLDE. Don't tell me signs. Don't tell me nightmares. My Hodel and that—that appetite.

TEVYA. When I tell what happened, you'll see it's a blessing from God. You remember you sent me to Ephraim? On the way I'm thinking, Under your very nose, Tevya; as is written, Beware the stranger in your own house ——

GOLDE. Don't tell me quotations!

TEVYA. So in the wagon I see, on the road, two heads—so close they look like one. (*Tevya moves to the side of the stage, re-enacting the scene. As before, he relates first to Golde, then to Hodel and Feferal.*) Then I see it's Hodel and Feferal. I approach. I observe. I frown. Hodel throws her arms around me. (*Hodel and Feferal approach Tevya. Their manner is sweet but determined, the exact opposite of Tevya's version as told to Golde.*)

HODEL. Congratulate us, papa.

TEVYA. (*To Hodel.*) Why? You found gold buried in the woods.

FEFERAL. Something better than that, Reb Tevya.

HODEL. We're engaged, papa.

GOLDE. She threw her arms around you, then?

TEVYA. (*Preoccupied with Hodel for the moment.*) What?

GOLDE. You frowned; she threw her arms around you—then?

TEVYA. (*To Golde.*) Exactly. She sought my protection, my blessing, papa, she said, I have something to ask of you.

GOLDE. Hodel asked?

TEVYA. She pleaded.

HODEL. (*Flatly and simply.*) We're going to be married, papa.

TEVYA. (*To Golde.*) She begged. (*He turns to Hodel.*) Just like that, you're going to be married. Without a match-maker, without arrangements, without even a discussion with the father in the case?

FEFERAL. What is there to discuss?

TEVYA. (*To Hodel, deferentially.*) First of all, if I'm entitled to an opinion, can I ask a question?

HODEL. Of course, papa.

TEVYA. How you'll live I won't ask. It's well-known that in love food is never mentioned. But, Feferal, I invited you into my house. We talked. You ate my wife's cooking. Now, without one word to an old man, you're getting married.

HODEL. We told you as soon as we decided.

FEFERAL. Would you rather we didn't tell you at all?

TEVYA. No, I'm delighted you confided in me—now that it's all settled. What about the terms?

FEFERAL. What's the sense of talking terms, Reb Tevya? I have nothing. You know that.

HODEL. We don't want anything, papa.

TEVYA. Such arrangements will make your mother dance.

GOLDE. So what are the terms?

TEVYA. (*To Golde, improvising as he proceeds.*) The terms are —his aunt in Yehupetz gives them her house. Two floors including furniture, dishes, linens, everything ——

GOLDE. Perchick, the cigarette-maker, has a rich sister in Yehupetz?

TEVYA. Not Perchick's sister. On his mother's side. That sister.

GOLDE. That sister not only isn't rich, on that side there is no sister.

TEVYA. An aunt, I forget. A great-aunt. Once-removed. What's the difference?

HODEL. It's all settled. We won't starve and we have each other.

TEVYA. So humble they were. On their knees to me. Get up, I said. Don't grovel in the dust before your father. Tevya has heard your plea. You agree to my terms. Therefore, they'll be a wedding such as Anatevka has never seen.

HODEL. Only the simplest ceremony, papa.

TEVYA. (*To Hodel.*) At least, thank God, there'll be a wedding. (*Hodel and Jeferal walk off. To Golde, now.*) Oh, there'll be such a wedding, Golde. Such challah—a golden loaf; such music, a celebration for two days ——

GOLDE. (*Interrupting.*) On his mother's side—that aunt? On their knees they were to you? Enough ——

TEVYA. (*In high dudgeon.*) You're questioning my words? If what I said is not the truth and the whole truth, may He who sits on high —— (*He stops.*)

GOLDE. Finish. Go, finish. (*A pause.*) All right. Now listen to me, my arranger. You'll end it now. This minute.

TEVYA. How?

GOLDE. You're not the father? She's not the daughter?

TEVYA. This is Hodel—who takes after you.

GOLDE. You'll open your mouth, without a quotation for once, and say No.

TEVYA. They love each other.

GOLDE. Let them hit their heads against a stone, they love each other. Your oldest married also—for love. But to my house she comes when she's hungry. And following behind her is the husband, the Tailor, as well.

TEVYA. What do you think I told them? You think I said Fine and halleluyah? I said you don't know what you're doing. I told them you'll starve. She looked at me with those eyes of hers. Papa, she said, we're going to be married. (*Gently, to Golde.*) Why do you think I said all right? Because, Golde, if not in front of us, then surely behind our backs they'll marry each other.

GOLDE. You slave for them. You break your back for them. They know better. And he makes stories for them.

TEVYA. I only know I'll see my Hodel a bride in the sight of God. There'll be a ceremony.

CHAVA. (*Entering.*) Papa, the rabbi is coming.

TEVYA. So put on another face. Don't upset the children. Our Hodel is a bride. She'll stand before a rabbi, thank God. Those

two, they would surely run off and get married alone. (*To Chava.*)
Tell them the ceremony is about to begin.

GOLDE. If I'll cry, believe me, it's not because I'm happy. (*Rabbi and his Wife enter. They are followed by Mottel and Tzeitl. Mottel plays his fiddle. There is general mazeltoving and greetings. Four small daughters enter, carrying a home-made chuppa, or marriage-canopy.*)

TEVYA. Mmm, fine. Out here. Bring the marriage canopy out under the open sky. Under God's eye. (*As he leads the little ones outdoors, he explains.*) The chuppa, the hope of a home, my children. Meaning, God willing, they'll have a roof over their heads, some of the time. (*Feferal enters "dressed" for the occasion.*)

FEFERAL. You promised, Reb Tevya; a simple ceremony.

TEVYA. (*Seeing Hodel approach.*) Behold. Behold the bride comes forth to meet the bridegroom. (*Hodel, accompanied by Golde, approaches the marriage canopy, wearing the traditional veil covering her face. Now a silence takes over. The Rabbi stands under the chuppa and the simple ceremony begins. It is the orthodox service for marriage without trimmings. The Rabbi occcupies a position* C.; *Feferal is at the Rabbi's* R. *Hodel at his* L.)

RABBI. Blessed art Thou, O Lord, Our God, who has created man in Thy image and woman out of his frame to stand beside him. (*Hodel circles Feferal three times.*) Oh, give abundant joy to these companions, even as Thou didst gladden Thy creation in the Garden of Eden. (*Rabbi hands Feferal a wine glass, as he speaks the blessing over the wine.*) Blessed art Thou, Lord, who bringeth forth the fruit of the vine. (*Feferal drinks, Hodel drinks from the same glass.*) And Adam said This is now bone of my bone and flesh of my flesh. And therefore shall a man leave his father and his mother and cleave unto his wife. And they shall be one flesh.

RABBI AND FEFERAL. (*In responsive reading.*) With this ring. (With this ring.) Be thou consecrated to me. (Be thou consecrated to me.) According to the laws of Moses and Israel. (According to the laws of Moses and Israel.) (*Feferal places the ring on her finger. Rabbi raises his hands in the final blessing.*)

RABBI. May there soon be heard in the land the songs of joyous wedding celebration, the sound of young people feasting and singing. Blessed art Thou, O Lord, who maketh the groom rejoice with the bride; who maketh this man and this woman, as one.

41

Step on the glass and break it. Amen. (*Feferal wraps the glass in a napkin and steps on it, breaking it. They kiss and the ceremony is over. Everyone gathers to congratulate them and Tevya and Golde.*)

AD LIBS. Mazeltov. Congratulations. Did you see how she went around him, turning his head already? (Ver-drehing his head, you mean.) Next year, a mazeltov. (Next year a bris.) (*Mottel's fiddle begins building behind—a song. A joyous celebration—a full wedding dance.*)

TEVYA. (*Overriding.*) Into the house, everyone. The wedding feast awaits. A little soup, a little challah, a little music —— (*Music leads everyone off except Hodel and Feferal—in embrace —and Tevya. He sees that Hodel is weeping.*) Behold, they didn't want a ceremony. Now their joy is overflowing. (*Hodel cries softly.*) Inside, my children. Everyone is waiting. This is the face of a bride one minute old? Tears.

HODEL. I don't know how to tell you, papa.

TEVYA. So I'll tell you. A thousand million did it before. But to every new bride after the ceremony it always looks dark.

FEFERAL. We should have told you before, but we didn't want to spoil the wedding. (*Tevya moves them off to the side, away from the house.*)

TEVYA. What is it? Speak.

FEFERAL. The reason we didn't want a celebration is—I have to leave.

TEVYA. You have to go?

FEFERAL. In a short time I have to go away.

TEVYA. And Hodel?

HODEL. I'll stay here till he sends for me.

TEVYA. (*Incredulous.*) The words have only just reached God's ears and you're parting from each other.

HODEL. We have to.

TEVYA. You stepped on a glass, my son. Do you know the meaning thereof? To remember the Destruction of the Temple (of course); but first to remember that a marriage is like a fine glass: be careful or you'll break it.

HODEL. This is Feferal's work. This is what he has to do.

TEVYA. He has to? Why? Where must you go? What must you do?

FEFERAL. I've said as much as I can.

42

TEVYA. Secrets now. More stupid secrets? Me you can't tell? Your father.

HODEL. You have to trust him, papa, and believe him ——

TEVYA. No. He'll tell me. He'll explain. What do you do? Where are you going? What is the secret you can't tell me?

FEFERAL. You know what I believe in. We've spoken of it many times.

TEVYA. Humanity, justice—that?

FEFERAL. (*Smiles.*) That.

TEVYA. Don't smile, my friend. Answer. This wonderful work you do, why is it such a terrible secret?

FEFERAL. Because they try to stop us.

TEVYA. Who tries to stop you?

HODEL. The Czar, his police.

TEVYA. Don't do it then. It's wrong, don't do it.

FEFERAL. It's not wrong. It has to be done.

TEVYA. What do you do? What? What good is all your talk if you can't tell a man like Tevya?

FEFERAL. We go among ordinary people. We ask questions. We try to show them the answer to their problems is in their own hands.

TEVYA. So go among the people here. We have ordinary people; we have problems. Your brother-in-law, the Tailor, is starving. Yerchmoil the Teacher—problems. There are hundreds here—all with troubles. Talk, ask, show, find a way to make a living and build your humanity in Anatevka.

FEFERAL. I can't. We go where we think we can do the most good.

TEVYA. Words, words. No sense.

FEFERAL. I've tried to tell you there is more to the world than your little patch of earth here. There are factories and farms and cities ——

TEVYA. You love the world, it's understood. You believe in justice in the factories, wonderful. You wallow in good deeds ——

HODEL. Papa!

TEVYA. I'll finish. This is your *principles* as you call it. But in life you marry my daughter and now you'll desert her. Listen to someone old enough to be your father. Someone who loves you. Someone who is your father. Tevya's world is Tevya's daughters. For this important world what are you doing?

FEFERAL. I've tried to tell you.

TEVYA. No, talk only about this much of the world. (*His arms encompass Hodel and Feferal.*) Only so much.

FEFERAL. Our poor Russia is made up of a million worlds like Tevya's world. Daughters, fathers, families, who want what you want. To eat every day, to enjoy the fruit of their work, to live in peace.

TEVYA. So therefore separate?

FEFERAL. But this is denied. In his lifetimes a man gathers enough for his funeral. And sometimes not that. And the Little Father sits on high and takes. The food of our fields he takes for his table; our sons he takes for his wars; the Jew the Little Father takes and blesses with a ghetto or a pogrom.

TEVYA. This is life. This is how things stand since the first day of Creation.

FEFERAL. But why, Reb Tevya, why?

TEVYA. Because this is the way God made the world.

FEFERAL. No. God gave us intellects so we should ask questions. If enough questions are asked there will be answers.

TEVYA. This is the portion you bring my child?

HODEL. Try to understand us, Papa.

TEVYA. You stood before God under the marriage canopy, which is the hope of a home. You spoke God's words. Your own mouth said it: Be thou consecrated unto me acccording to the laws of Moses and Israel. What is the law: to love, to walk humbly, to be one flesh, to create life—l'chaim. If you go, you go without my blessing. (*He hears the strains of the wedding music from within.*) Go in the house. They'll be running out in a minute wondering where you are. (*Feferal and Hodel go in as Golde appears.*)

GOLDE. I heard. You come inside too. At such a time it's better to be together. (*The sound of the fiddle is heard, soaring.*)

TEVYA. Is there anything in the world like the sound of a fiddle at a Jewish wedding? (*He walks toward Golde and the house. SLOW FADE OUT. LIGHTS SLOWLY FADE ON to reveal a warm September twilight outside Tevya's house. It is six weeks later. Tevya is alone, building a succah, or small booth made of leafy branches.*) Tonight is six weeks, dear Lord, since Hodel has not seen her Feferal Perchick and tonight is the seventh day of the Feast of Succoth, a holiday of joy. Tonight we celebrate the

44

blessings of Thy harvest, and remembering Thy bounty, we erect a succcah, a booth, made of the branches of Thy trees. (*He adds a few branches.*) This is the night we call Hashonah Rabbo, when the heavens open and each man can make his plea to You directly. Bless, then, my family and my Golde, my daughters and their husbands. And for Hodel, comfort her and answer her prayers. (*Hodel enters and stands watching Tevya. There is a brief silence as he adds the last branches.*)

HODEL. (*Frightened by the news and the prospects, but braving it as well as she can.*) I have news, papa.

TEVYA. If you want to tell me, fine. If not, Tevya can wait. What?

HODEL. I know where he's been all this time.

TEVYA. If you want to, speak.

HODEL. He's far away. He's serving time.

TEVYA. They arrested him? For his good deeds they locked him in a prison?

HODEL. They're sending him away—to Siberia.

TEVYA. To the far reaches of the North?

HODEL. (*Nodding.*) This is good-bye, papa. Tomorrow morning, I'm going to join him. I may never see you again.

TEVYA. Do you know what you're saying? You'll go after him?! Do you know what it's like in the far wastes where Alexander of Macedonia, the great explorer, where even he was trapped there by icy savages?

HODEL. Papa, I have to be with him.

TEVYA. Who ever heard of a young girl marrying a man so she could follow him—into exile?

HODEL. Papa, it's bad enough ——

TEVYA. What shall I do? Fall on your neck and plead with you? Shall I tie you with a rope? Go. Tell your mother good-bye and go. Travel to the other end of the earth where it's forever frozen and there isn't a Jew for a thousand miles. (*Hodel cries.*) This is the bed you made, go lie in it. (*Hodel moves away, struck by the rejection. Tevya has turned from her. Now he faces her, sees her plight, moves toward her with open arms. They embrace.*)

HODEL. (*Her head in his arms.*) Oh, papa, I'm so unhappy.

TEVYA. What then? This news should make us celebrate? (*Gently he leads her to the doorstep of the house and both sit.*) It's crowded a little. Well, crowding is a Jewish custom. If no

45

one crowds us, we crowd ourselves. (*A pause.*) There's a story in the Midrash ——
HODEL. What, papa?
TEVYA. Nah, a lot of words.
HODEL. Tell me.
TEVYA. A story. Once there was a hen and she hatched out some ducks. (Not chicks, you understand, but ducks.) So the hen taught them and fed them and raised them until they grew big enough and they took to the water. And there was the hen on the shore, clucking after the ducks—but the ducks only swam away. What do you say to that?
HODEL. I feel sorry for the hen, but just because she stood there clucking, should the ducks have stopped swimming?
TEVYA. Therefore the hen has a few words to say. To the duck. You took a pledge before God my daughter. Under God's eye. You and your Matchstick. What does it mean:—Therefore shall a daughter leave her father and her mother and cling to her husband?
HODEL. Can I do that, papa?
TEVYA. You can. The meaning thereof is Go. Wherever he is this is your place. Whatever trouble, however cold. Look in your own face, you'll have your answer. For six weeks he's gone, for six weeks the color is gone from your face. You eat, you breathe, but you're not alive. You walk like the moon through the sky. Pale and without life. In your mind you're with him already.
HODEL. I'm afraid.
TEVYA. Be afraid. It's permitted. Only a fool is not afraid and the daughters of Tevya are not fools. You'll be together. You'll see him whenever they let you. You'll whisper, you'll laugh, you'll cry—but you'll be together.
HODEL. Can I do that?
TEVYA. You can and more. How will it be? I'll paint you the picture. (You'll see your father talked a lot, but also listened.) He'll serve his time; you'll wait. Meanwhile the pot is boiling, as they say. Then one day (When? One day.)—it happens and the sun will rise and everything will be bright and shining. Then he'll be free with all the others like him and together you'll roll up your sleeves and turn the Little Father upside down.
HODEL. It's what I want to believe, so much.
TEVYA. Believe it. To Tevya the prospect is not exactly marvellous, but what does Tevya know? Tevya knows only his daugh-

46

ters. And the daughters of Tevya, when they love, they love with their heads, their hearts, their bodies and their souls. With everything. Could Hodel be Hodel any other way?

HODEL. Papa, I think maybe you've given me the strength to try it.

TEVYA. You had it all along. Maybe it got lost along the road somewheres. But you had it. So go. Tell your Matchstick in the wilds, your Alexander in the frozen wastes, that Tevya commands him to take care of my child. Tell him I rely on him as a man of honor. Tell him, also, I send him more than my blessing—I send my daughter. And once in a while, write your old Papa and tell him you're both alive. (*Hodel cries, and kisses Tevya.*) No tears. It's forbidden. Tonight is the night of Hashonah Rabbo, when our fate is sealed with our God. A holy day and therefore it's a sin to cry. (*He leads Hodel into the house.*) Go, pack. For such a journey you'll need more than strength. A few warm blankets will help. (*Hodel goes. Alone.*) So, the Lord in heaven, wished to grant merit in Israel, and therefore He gave to Tevya seven daughters. Like Esther in the Bible, fair of form and beautiful to look upon. Also proud and high-spirited. And as if that weren't bad enough, they have to have brains, too. So Tevya has now concluded two happy arrangements and there are five to come. My Chava, my next, has begun with a writer: a second Gorki, she tells me. Although who the first Gorki is I never heard. How they live, these writers, I haven't yet discovered. Maybe they eat pages. The name of this writer is—Fedka Galaghan: not exactly a Jewish name. So what will happen there, I leave to your tender mercies. My little ones are too young to be problems; but they'll grow into it. (*He laughs.*) You know what I'm thinking, O Lord. I'm thinking, Tevya leave the management of the Universe to God. I have my own work to do. Besides I talk too much. Good night. (*As he walks toward the house, LIGHTS FADE OUT.*)

CURTAIN

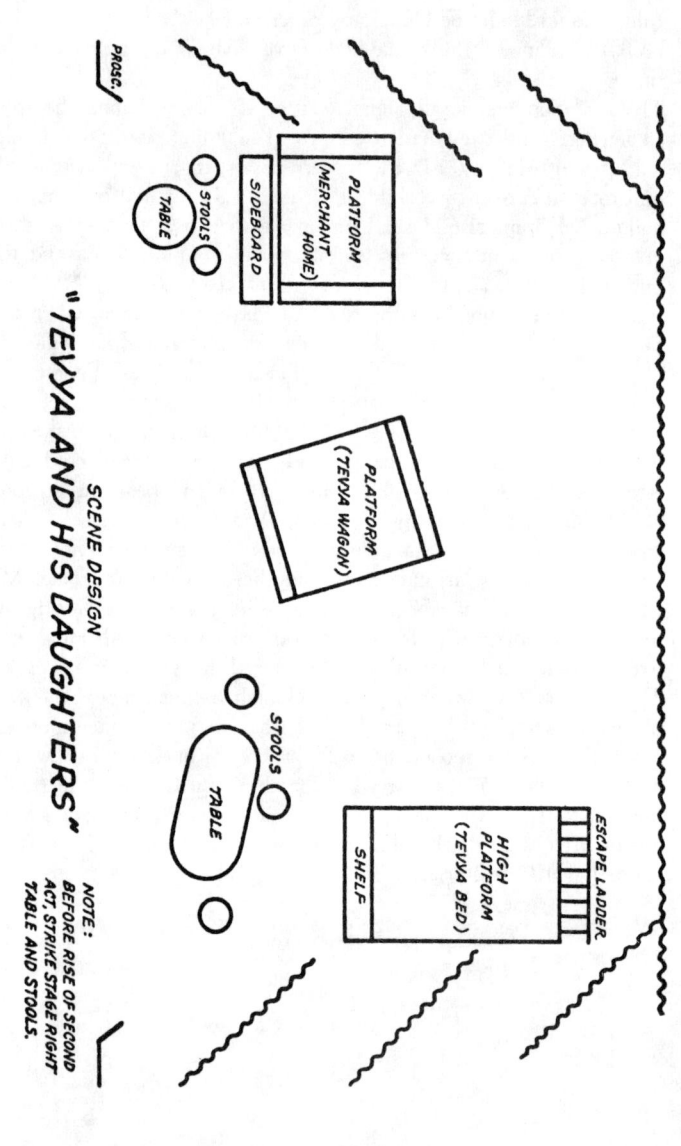

SCENE DESIGN
"TEVYA AND HIS DAUGHTERS"

PROSC.

PLATFORM
(MERCHANT
HOME)

SIDEBOARD

STOOLS

TABLE

PLATFORM
(TEVYA WAGON)

STOOLS

TABLE

HIGH
PLATFORM
(TEVYA BED)

SHELF

ESCAPE LADDER

NOTE:
BEFORE RISE OF SECOND
ACT, STRIKE STAGE RIGHT
TABLE AND STOOLS.

SUGGESTIONS FOR STAGING

NOTES ON LIGHTING

Act I:

It is suggested that four main areas of lighting be used: Tevya's house, the wagon and road, Lazar Wolf's house, the Rich Merchant's area. Although the areas should be demarked, there is no need to keep action confined to the areas, which roughly are s. L. for Tevya's house, c. s. for the wagon, D. s. R. for Lazar Wolf's and u. s. R. for Rich Merchant's.

During the story-telling episodes in Act I—Part 1 and in Act II, Tevya can and does move freely in and out of the house area, the Merchant's area and the road—now expanding, now contracting the scene as he chooses. Fluidity would be the key here.

In Act II, there are two areas, which sometimes overlap. Interior of Tevya's house is (as before) s. L. The rest of the stage constitutes the "outdoors," where the wedding takes place, where Tevya encounters Feferal, where Tevya meets Hodel and Feferal, where he says good-bye to Hodel.

There should be no suggestion of walls confining Tevya's house. Nor any convention of doors. Entrances and exits are made irrespective of this kind of realism.

The light cues follow:

Act I—Part 1:

1. Pre-set. (Where a curtain is used, when the curtain is raised or opened, the pre-set will be revealed. But the show can be performed without a curtain. In that case the following pre-set is seen by the audience when they arrive and before the play starts.) Tevya arrives on the stage at midnight. Exterior of the house needs one light as Tevya speaks his opening prayer. House is dimly lit—nearly black. (P. 5)

2. On Tevya's line "Let there be light" lights slowly come up on interior of Tevya's house. (P. 5) In the course of the scene, the light is enhanced by candles till it is up full by Tevya's line "Behold—soup with noodles." (P. 6)

3. As Tevya begins to relate his story, (p. 7) lights dim slightly on his home, come up on the area of his wagon. With the arrival of the Rich Women, the wagon area is increased to include most of c. and s. R. (P. 8)

4. As the Merchant appears on his porch, lights come up fully on u. s. R. area. (P. 10)

49

5. As Tevya takes leave of the Merchant, lights gently fade on Merchant and come up in Tevya's house to where they were at Cue 2. (P. 11)

6. The Fadeout is slow and gentle. (P. 13)

Act I—Part 2:

7. Lights fade in on c. s. —Tevya's wagon. Rest of the stage remains unlit. (P. 13)

8. Tevya leaves his wagon to enter Lazar Wolf's, as lights come on slowly to illuminate D. S. R. area: Lazar Wolf's. (P. 14)

9. The Lazar Wolf scene ends with laughter and a Fadeout, which never quite goes to black. Instead there is a crossfade with the exterior area. Tevya weave-dances through this into his home, which lights up slowly as Golde enters, last line. (P. 18)

10. The wagon-shed where Tevya begins his scene with Tzeitl is D. S. L., in the Lazar Wolf area, played in total disregard of chairs and table present. It now simply functions as Tevya's barn. The area is lit with Tevya's arrival on the line "So, my Tzeitl, come to your papa's arms." (P. 22)

11. Mottel's entrance calls for fuller illumination of the s. R. area, u. and D. s. (P. 23)

12. Lights fade to black at end of the scene. (P. 24)

13. Tevya's screams bring up the lights slowly. (P. 24) As his daughters enter, candles in hand, the lights come up more fully. The effect, however, is light at midnight—never bright. (P. 25)

14. Lights fade as Golde and Tevya settle back in bed, go to very dim with Tzeitl's exit, and on Tevya's last line, lingeringly fade out for curtain. (P. 27)

Act II:

1. Light reveals Tevya, again in his wagon. The day is sunny, the effect hot. (P. 28)

2. At close of Feferal scene, lights fade. (P. 32)

3. Eating scene begins with lights suddenly illuminating the Tevya house, particularly the kitchen table. It is night. (P. 32)

4. Scene ends with a slow fadeout. (P. 37)

5. The "wedding scene" begins as did the play. Tevya again revealed outside his house; then as he enters lights illuminate the interior. (P. 37)

6. As Tevya re-enacts the encounter with Feferal and Hodel c. (wagon) lights come on, as do D. s. R. area, where Hodel and Feferal stand. Most of the lighting is on the apron, the place of action. (P. 38)

7. As Hodel and Feferal walk off, lights in their area remain, as do

the wagon-light—but when the wedding begins, all lights come up several points, taking in the entire stage. (P. 40)

8. Scene ends with slow fade out to black. This denotes a passage of time, six weeks. (P. 44)

9. Lights fade on slowly to suggest autumn evening sunlight. (P. 44)

10. Lights fade slowly out as Tevya walks toward his house. (P. 47)

NOTES ON COSTUMES

Costumes, generally, are Middle European, turn-of-the-century, rural, peasant clothes. Although the clothes of Tevya, Golde and his daughters are poor, home-made and have a well-worn and well-washed look, they do not lack for color. The entire play is costumed in rich, warm tones, the only cool note is introduced in a deep purple (or black) to set Feferal apart as a student. The Rich People, representative of the leisure class of the time, should be citified, show the influence of Paris and St. Petersburg in the clothing they wear.

Tevya wears rust-colored pants of homespun material. Well-worn brown leather boots and apron, peasant shirt (full-sleeved and round-necked) with no collar—open at the throat. He wears a black visor hat (over his yarmalka), typical of Jews of the period. His "transformation" to a Dairyman is accomplished by removing the heavy leather drayman's apron, and substituting an apron of light colored heavy muslin.

Golde and the Three Daughters wear floor length peasant skirts and contrasting peasant blouses, the younger the daughter the shorter the skirt. They wear aprons and babushkas as the situation demands. The materials are calico prints of varying hues. A suggested color arrangement is: Golde in warm browns and golds; Hodel in pinks, reds and oranges; Tzeitl in blues, blue-greens and lavenders; Chava in yellows and blues.

Lazar Wolf wears work boots, dark-materialed work pants, a faded magenta shirt with no collar, a white (stained) full length butcher's apron. Yarmalka.

Mottel, poor and threadbare, in olive drab pants, eggshell shirt, misshapen cap and rimless glasses.

Rich Woman wears a lavender print, period dress with full lace bodice and sleeves, lavender lace draped veil, beaded drawstring bag and white lace gloves. Her daughter in lime-green printed princess floor length dress, with full back. She carries a shocking pink, lace trimmed parasol, lace gloves and a drawstring bag.

The Rich Merchant wears gaiters, elegantly cut black slim period pants, white period shirt, black satin tie, and a heavily brocaded double-breasted vest with gold watch chain. Arm garters.

TEVYA, GOLDE and his DAUGHTERS wear variations of beige, and yellow cotton flannel nightgowns for the sleeping scenes.

FEFERAL wears black student's boots, royal blue pants, and a Russian peasant blouse in purple. He wears a gray-blue student's cap. Carries a purple jacket.

For the wedding scene, Golde throws a lace shawl over her head. Hodel wears two lace shawls, arranged so that her head, face and shoulders are covered. The Rabbi wears the traditional orthodox black kaftan, with wide-brimmed high-crowned felt hat, and tallis. All others attending the ceremony add bright touches to their attire.

PROPERTY LIST

ACT I

Offstage R.:
Two platters with food (Tevya)
Wine bottle (Tevya)
Two faked platters of food (Rich Woman)
Rubles (Tevya and Rich Merchant)
Offstage L.:
Candlesticks with candles (girls and Golde)
Matches
On Stage:
Brass samovar, sugar, silver goblet, schnapps decanter, small cup for schnapps, glass of tea, spread of food, all these on S. R. sideboard
Pewter samovar, assorted cups and plates, eating utensils, tablecloth, brown paper and pencil, all these on S. L. shelf

ACT II

Offstage R.:
Paper bound book (Feferal)
Chuppa
Trees for Succah
Napkin (Rabbi)
On Stage:
Small schnapps glass on S. R. sideboard
Plate and fork on S. L. table, plate with latkes, two glasses tea, napkin with latkes, brown paper and pencil for marriage contract, all these on S. L. shelf

(NOTE on the marriage canopy [chuppah] and booth of branches [succah]: The marriage canopy can consist of two upright branches with leaves or a small branch extending from one side. With the branches turned outward and a strip of velvet material joining the two uprights, a satisfactory marriage canopy can be produced. Removing the velvet material, and turning the branches in toward each other —a succah is formed.)

MUSIC CUES
(See note on copyright page)

Act I

1. Overture. House dims to half and the Overture is played. (P. 5)

2. House is dark and Tevya's Theme begins. It is faded behind his opening speech. (P. 5)

3. Close of Scene 1, after Tevya's line: "Then Tevya the Dairyman begins a new life"; simultaneous with the fadeout. This music segues into Tevya's theme which carries us through the fade in to Tevya in his wagon. The music fades behind his remarks to his horse, fades out by the third sentence. (P. 13)

4. Close of Lazar Wolf scene, music dances Tevya home slightly drunk. If Tevya can, let him hum or sing a Rosh Hashonah song here. (P. 18)

5. The Mottel scene ends with a slow fade and music. The music is transitional to Tevya asleep above the oven. Music continues until Tevya cuts it off with his shout: "No. Help! Stop. No!" (P. 24)

6. Music sneaks in behind dialogue with Tzeitl's "Good night, Mama. Good night, Papa." Continues behind and then is up full after Tevya's comment, "Meaning Tevya is a little bit of a liar." (P. 27)

Act II

7. An entr'acte begins Act II. It is played with the house at half. (P. 28)

8. When house is dark and prior to lights revealing Tevya in his wagon music is stated, then backs Tevya's second comments to his horse, fading out as before (Cue 3). (P. 28)

9. The Feferal scene ends in fadeout. Music now bursts in—setting the stage for the argument that follows. (P. 32)

10. A slow light fade ends the arguing scene. A short, prayerlike cue introduces Tevya outside his house. The music backs his speech beginning: "You know what you're doing, O Lord . . ." and fades out. (P. 37)

11. Golde's line "If I cry, believe me it's not because I'm happy" brings on the wedding music. It builds behind the action and dialogue —until it fades out just before the ceremony itself begins. (P. 41)

12. With the last line of the ceremony "Step on the glass and break it. Amen"—there is general congratulations and a burst of wedding music. Everyone dances, a peasants' dance, to the full, spirited musical

statement. It sustains until Tevya moves everyone into the house. Then it is heard only faintly behind the scene between Tevya, Hodel and Feferal. Music should be out by Hodel's "I don't know how to tell you, papa." (P. 42)

13. Tevya's speech "If you go, you go without my blessing" brings back the strains of music at the party within the house (i.e. off-stage). The music remains subdued for his next speech and Golde's, then soars and fades before his final speech: "Is there anything in the world like the sound of a fiddle . . . ?" (P. 44)

14. Music is heard in the darkness between scenes. It backs Tevya's remarks beginning with the words "Tonight is six weeks, dear Lord . . ." and goes out on "made of the branches of Thy trees." (P. 44)

15. Music fades in slowly with Tevya's comment to Hodel, "No tears. It is forbidden." It backs the rest of his speech through the end of the play—gently behind. It rises only as Tevya gestures Good night to God. (P. 47)

16. The finale music may be played as the audience exits.

(NOTE: It may be helpful to listen to the music cues on the Columbia Masterwork of TEVYA AND HIS DAUGHTERS. Music in this album is used essentially as it should be in the play.)

NEW PLAYS

★ **BE AGGRESSIVE by Annie Weisman.** Vista Del Sol is paradise, sandy beaches, avocado-lined streets. But for seventeen-year-old cheerleader Laura, everything changes when her mother is killed in a car crash, and she embarks on a journey to the Spirit Institute of the South where she can learn "cheer" with Bible belt intensity. "...filled with lingual gymnastics...stylized rapid-fire dialogue..." –*Variety*. "...a new, exciting, and unique voice in the American theatre..." –*BackStage West*. [1M, 4W, extras] ISBN: 0-8222-1894-1

★ **FOUR by Christopher Shinn.** Four people struggle desperately to connect in this quiet, sophisticated, moving drama. "...smart, broken-hearted...Mr. Shinn has a precocious and forgiving sense of how power shifts in the game of sexual pursuit...He promises to be a playwright to reckon with..." –*NY Times*. "A voice emerges from an American place. It's got humor, sadness and a fresh and touching rhythm that tell of the loneliness and secrets of life...[a] poetic, haunting play." –*NY Post*. [3M, 1W] ISBN: 0-8222-1850-X

★ **WONDER OF THE WORLD by David Lindsay-Abaire.** A madcap picaresque involving Niagara Falls, a lonely tour-boat captain, a pair of bickering private detectives and a husband's dirty little secret. "Exceedingly whimsical and playfully wicked. Winning and genial. A top-drawer production." –*NY Times*. "Full frontal lunacy is on display. A most assuredly fresh and hilarious tragicomedy of marital discord run amok...absolutely hysterical..." –*Variety*. [3M, 4W (doubling)] ISBN: 0-8222-1863-1

★ **QED by Peter Parnell.** Nobel Prize-winning physicist and all-around genius Richard Feynman holds forth with captivating wit and wisdom in this fascinating biographical play that originally starred Alan Alda. "QED is a seductive mix of science, human affections, moral courage, and comic eccentricity. It reflects on, among other things, death, the absence of God, travel to an unexplored country, the pleasures of drumming, and the need to know and understand." –*NY Magazine*. "Its rhythms correspond to the way that people—even geniuses—approach and avoid highly emotional issues, and it portrays Feynman with affection and awe." –*The New Yorker*. [1M, 1W] ISBN: 0-8222-1924-7

★ **UNWRAP YOUR CANDY by Doug Wright.** Alternately chilling and hilarious, this deliciously macabre collection of four bedtime tales for adults is guaranteed to keep you awake for nights on end. "Engaging and intellectually satisfying...a treat to watch." –*NY Times*. "Fiendishly clever. Mordantly funny and chilling. Doug Wright teases, freezes and zaps us." –*Village Voice*. "Four bite-size plays that bite back." –*Variety*. [flexible casting] ISBN: 0-8222-1871-2

★ **FURTHER THAN THE FURTHEST THING by Zinnie Harris.** On a remote island in the middle of the Atlantic secrets are buried. When the outside world comes calling, the islanders find their world blown apart from the inside as well as beyond. "Harris winningly produces an intimate and poetic, as well as political, family saga." –*Independent (London)*. "Harris' enthralling adventure of a play marks a departure from stale, well-furrowed theatrical terrain." –*Evening Standard (London)*. [3M, 2W] ISBN: 0-8222-1874-7

★ **THE DESIGNATED MOURNER by Wallace Shawn.** The story of three people living in a country where what sort of books people like to read and how they choose to amuse themselves becomes both firmly personal and unexpectedly entangled with questions of survival. "This is a playwright who does not just tell you what it is like to be arrested at night by goons or to fall morally apart and become an aimless yet weirdly contented ghost yourself. He has the originality to make you feel it." –*Times (London)*. "A fascinating play with beautiful passages of writing..." –*Variety*. [2M, 1W] ISBN: 0-8222-1848-8

DRAMATISTS PLAY SERVICE, INC.
440 Park Avenue South, New York, NY 10016 212-683-8960 Fax 212-213-1539
postmaster@dramatists.com   www.dramatists.com

NEW PLAYS

★ **SHEL'S SHORTS by Shel Silverstein.** Lauded poet, songwriter and author of children's books, the incomparable Shel Silverstein's short plays are deeply infused with the same wicked sense of humor that made him famous. "...[a] childlike honesty and twisted sense of humor." –*Boston Herald.* "...terse dialogue and an absurdity laced with a tang of dread give [*Shel's Shorts*] more than a trace of Samuel Beckett's comic existentialism." –*Boston Phoenix.* [flexible casting] ISBN: 0-8222-1897-6

★ **AN ADULT EVENING OF SHEL SILVERSTEIN by Shel Silverstein.** Welcome to the darkly comic world of Shel Silverstein, a world where nothing is as it seems and where the most innocent conversation can turn menacing in an instant. These ten imaginative plays vary widely in content, but the style is unmistakable. "...[*An Adult Evening*] shows off Silverstein's virtuosic gift for wordplay...[and] sends the audience out...with a clear appreciation of human nature as perverse and laughable." –*NY Times.* [flexible casting] ISBN: 0-8222-1873-9

★ **WHERE'S MY MONEY? by John Patrick Shanley.** A caustic and sardonic vivisection of the institution of marriage, laced with the author's inimitable razor-sharp wit. "...Shanley's gift for acid-laced one-liners and emotionally tumescent exchanges is certainly potent..." –*Variety.* "...lively, smart, occasionally scary and rich in reverse wisdom." –*NY Times.* [3M, 3W] ISBN: 0-8222-1865-8

★ **A FEW STOUT INDIVIDUALS by John Guare.** A wonderfully screwy comedy-drama that figures Ulysses S. Grant in the throes of writing his memoirs, surrounded by a cast of fantastical characters, including the Emperor and Empress of Japan, the opera star Adelina Patti and Mark Twain. "Guare's smarts, passion and creativity skyrocket to awesome heights..." –*Star Ledger.* "...precisely the kind of good new play that you might call an everyday miracle...every minute of it is fresh and newly alive..." –*Village Voice.* [10M, 3W] ISBN: 0-8222-1907-7

★ **BREATH, BOOM by Kia Corthron.** A look at fourteen years in the life of Prix, a Bronx native, from her ruthless girl-gang leadership at sixteen through her coming to maturity at thirty. "...vivid world, believable and eye-opening, a place worthy of a dramatic visit, where no one would want to live but many have to." –*NY Times.* "...rich with humor, terse vernacular strength and gritty detail..." –*Variety.* [1M, 9W] ISBN: 0-8222-1849-6

★ **THE LATE HENRY MOSS by Sam Shepard.** Two antagonistic brothers, Ray and Earl, are brought together after their father, Henry Moss, is found dead in his seedy New Mexico home in this classic Shepard tale. "...His singular gift has been for building mysteries out of the ordinary ingredients of American family life..." –*NY Times.* "...rich moments ...Shepard finds gold." –*LA Times.* [7M, 1W] ISBN: 0-8222-1858-5

★ **THE CARPETBAGGER'S CHILDREN by Horton Foote.** One family's history spanning from the Civil War to WWII is recounted by three sisters in evocative, intertwining monologues. "...bittersweet music—[a] rhapsody of ambivalence...in its modest, garrulous way...theatrically daring." –*The New Yorker.* [3W] ISBN: 0-8222-1843-7

★ **THE NINA VARIATIONS by Steven Dietz.** In this funny, fierce and heartbreaking homage to *The Seagull*, Dietz puts Chekhov's star-crossed lovers in a room and doesn't let them out. "A perfect little jewel of a play..." –*Shepherdstown Chronicle.* "...a delightful revelation of a writer at play; and also an odd, haunting, moving theater piece of lingering beauty." –*Eastside Journal (Seattle).* [1M, 1W (flexible casting)] ISBN: 0-8222-1891-7

DRAMATISTS PLAY SERVICE, INC.
440 Park Avenue South, New York, NY 10016 212-683-8960 Fax 212-213-1539
postmaster@dramatists.com www.dramatists.com